TAKE CONTROL OF ASPERGER'S SYNDROME

TAKE CONTROL OF ASPERGER'S SYNDROME

The Official Strategy Guide for Teens With Asperger's Syndrome and Nonverbal Learning Disorder

Janet Price and
Jennifer Engel Fisher

PRUFROCK PRESS INC.
WACO, TEXAS

Library of Congress Cataloging-in-Publication Data

Price, Janet, 1964-
Take control of Asperger's syndrome : the official strategy guide for teens with Asperger's syndrome and non-verbal learning disorder / Janet Price and Jennifer Engel Fisher.
  p. cm.
Includes bibliographical references.
ISBN-13: 978-1-59363-405-6 (pbk.)
ISBN-10: 1-59363-405-6 (pbk.)
1. Asperger's syndrome in children--Patients--Life skills guides 2. Asperger's syndrome in adolescence--Patients--Life skills guides. 3. Nonverbal learning disabilities--Patients--Life skills guides 4. Self-care, Health. I. Fisher, Jennifer Engel, 1970- II. Title.
RJ506.A9P755 2010
618.92'858832--dc22
                    2009050852

Copyright © 2010, Prufrock Press Inc.
Edited by Lacy Compton
Cover and Layout Design by Marjorie Parker
Author photo by D. Goozh Kesterman.

ISBN-13: 978-1-59363-405-6
ISBN-10: 1-59363-405-6

Printed in the United States of America.

At the time of this book's publication, all facts and figures cited are the most current available. All telephone numbers, addresses, and Web site URLs are accurate and active. All publications, organizations, websites, and other resources exist as described in the book, and all have been verified. The authors and Prufrock Press Inc. make no warranty or guarantee concerning the information and materials given out by organizations or content found at websites, and we are not responsible for any changes that occur after this book's publication. If you find an error, please contact Prufrock Press Inc.

Prufrock Press Inc.
P.O. Box 8813
Waco, TX 76714-8813
Phone: (800) 998-2208
Fax: (800) 240-0333
http://www.prufrock.com

DEDICATION

I dedicate this book to my husband Richard, whose love, support, and unswerving belief in me makes all things possible; to my children, Benjamin and Lauren, who inspire me every day; and to the entire Price clan, where I look to when I need strategies of my own.

—Janet

I dedicate this book to my husband Noel, whose commitment to my vision and success allowed this book to come to fruition; to my amazing children Ethan and Brett, who have been so patient throughout this process and can't wait to see their names in print; and my parents, Sandor and Sue Engel for always believing in me.

—Jennifer

CONTENTS

ACKNOWLEDGMENTS

There are many dedicated professionals and friends whose support along the way has been invaluable.

First and foremost, we wish to thank Rich Weinfeld, our colleague, mentor, and friend, without whom this book would not have been possible. We are grateful for the continued friendship and support of all of the members of the Weinfeld Education Group.

We also wish to thank our editor, Lacy Compton, for her support throughout this process.

A special thank you to Dr. Paula Elitov, for her help and encouragement throughout the years, and guidance in this project.

We thank John Howard at the Springstone School in Lafayette, CA, for supporting us early on and allowing us to survey his students.

We also thank the participants on the NLD Internet message board at Delphi Forums, for their contributions and anecdotes. A special thank you to Trish Simpson and Karen Randall, who moderate the NLD message board with Janet Price.

We are grateful to Katie Miller for allowing us to interview her about her strengths and passions, and congratulate her on recently being named a recipient of the Wynn Newhouse Award for artists with disabilities. Thanks also goes to all of the teenagers and young adults across the country who took the time to speak with us, e-mail us, or participate in our survey to share their experiences about Asperger's syndrome and Nonverbal Learning Disorder.

We also gratefully acknowledge all those who paved the road ahead of us—the researchers, writers, and practitioners in the fields of Asperger's syndrome and Nonverbal Learning Disorder. We wish to extend special thanks to Pamela Tanguay, Joan Scott, and Rondalyn Varney Whitney for furthering the understanding of Nonverbal Learning Disorder. Those of us in the NLD community would surely not be where we are today, if these women were not courageous, insightful, and generous enough to share their very personal experiences.

FOREWORD

The authors have accomplished their mission! Janet Price and Jennifer Engel Fisher give you, students who have been diagnosed with Asperger's syndrome or Nonverbal Learning Disorder, a very clear guidebook for how to achieve success. They do so in a way that clearly respects the wonderful strengths that you already demonstrate every day. The authors learned about what works for teens like you from their years of experience in the classroom, as parents of children like you, as advocates for many other students who are similar to you, as trainers of teachers who work with students like you, and as consultants to schools and school districts that work with you. They know that you can and will be successful as students and adults. The message that underlies every strategy that they present to you is that there is nothing wrong with you as you are. The strategies that you will learn by reading this book aren't going to change you into someone else; rather, they will empower you to fully realize your own unique potential.

This book will also let you know that you're not alone—far from it. Ms. Price and Ms. Fisher share the results of surveys of teens like you about what they love and what they hate; what works for them and what doesn't. The authors also share advice directly from individuals diagnosed with Asperger's syndrome or Nonverbal Learning Disorder, some of whom are still teens and others who are now adults and have vivid memories of their successes and struggles.

It is my belief that the most important strategy that you will learn from reading this book is the importance of self-advocacy. By understanding your own strengths and challenges and learning what will work for you, you will be armed with the information you need to fully access your education. You will be able to use the author's suggestions to speak to adults about what works for you and why. Speaking in this way will not only allow you to get what you need, it also will educate the adults in your life about who you are and how they can best help you. When you advocate for yourself, with the knowledge gained from reading this book, you also will find that adults will be more willing to go the extra mile as they partner with you in your best interest.

I think that you'll agree with me that this book is very clearly written and easy to use. Each chapter ends with a summary of key points that you can refer to as reminders of the strategies you can use. I think that you'll enjoy reading this book from cover to cover and then will want to keep it handy to check back with frequently.

I have had the wonderful opportunity to work with many students like you. I directed a school program for kids who were simultaneously gifted and had disabilities. Since then, I have advocated for many students like you, taught a graduate school course about kids and teens who learn like you, hosted a radio show focused on topics dealing with kids and teens just like you, and written several books for parents and educators about students like you. There are four major best practices that summarize what I know that smart students who learn differently need in their school programs:

1. *Appropriately rigorous and challenging instruction in the student's area of strength:* It is clear that if you are to succeed in life you will do so by capitalizing on your strengths.

Schools must provide an opportunity for students like you to identify and build on your strengths, to learn how these strengths connect to careers, and to utilize your strengths to overcome your weaknesses.

2. *Instruction of skills and strategies in academic areas that are affected by the student's disability*: We must help students like you to continue to develop all of your skills including social skills, organizational skills, reading comprehension skills, and written language skills.

3. *An appropriately differentiated program, including individualized instructional adaptations and accommodations systemically provided to students*: Appropriately selected adaptations and accommodations allow students like you to access the curriculum and utilize your strengths. Teachers and parents should always strive to help you move from dependence to independence, understand your own unique strengths and weaknesses, and learn to be a powerful self-advocate.

4. *Comprehensive case management to coordinate all aspects of the student's Individualized Education Program*: Each student needs a case manager in school who takes on the responsibility of making sure that students like you are both being challenged appropriately and receiving the appropriate supports. These case managers must be a mentor to the students they work with, develop a partnership with the parents, and communicate with all those in school and in the community who are working on behalf of these students.

As I described above, what I have been doing is attempting to teach parents and educators about how to work with students like you. What I love about *Take Control of Asperger's Syndrome: The Official Strategy Guide for Teens With Asperger's Syndrome and Nonverbal Learning Disorder* is that it is not a book written for parents and educators. It is a book written for you. But, do me and yourself a favor—talk to your parents and teachers about it. When they hear from you that these strategies really work, they will believe in them and that will make a huge difference not only for your but for the many other students who also have Asperger's syndrome and Nonverbal Learning Disorder. These students, like you, have the potential to do great things when the adults in their life allow them to use these powerful strategies.

So, go ahead and get started on the wonderful journey of self-discovery and achievement that will flow from reading and practicing the strategies in this book.

I am confident that you will accomplish your mission and take control of Asperger's syndrome and Nonverbal Learning Disorder!

Rich Weinfeld
Coauthor of the best-selling books *School Success for Kids With Asperger's Syndrome, Smart Kids With Learning Difficulties, Helping Boys Succeed in School,* and *Special Needs Advocacy Resource Book.*

INTRODUCTION

f you've picked up this book, then chances are either you or someone you know is living with Asperger's syndrome (AS) or Nonverbal Learning Disorder (NLD). These conditions greatly impact everyday life, but many people know nothing about them. Teachers, friends, or even family members may not understand why some things that seem easy for most people are not so easy for you. You may not understand why some people act the way they do or how to respond to them.

You may sometimes feel like you are all alone, but the truth is, if you are living with AS or NLD you are not the only one. In fact, a study conducted by Dr. Michael Kogan and his colleagues, published in *Pediatrics* in October 2009, indicated that 1 in every 91 American children is diagnosed with an autism spectrum disorder (AS is on the autism spectrum; NLD bears many autism spectrum-like characteristics). In December 2009, the Centers for Disease Control and Prevention reported that 1 in 110 children could be classified as having an autism spectrum disorder, a change from its 2007 estimate of 1 in 150. Furthermore, in

September 2009, England's National Health Service (NHS) released a study showing that autism rates among adults, all the way through their 70s, are roughly the same as those found in children worldwide, approximately 1 in 100 (see the *TIME* magazine article by Claudia Wallis at http://www.time.com/time/health/article/0,8599,1927415,00.html if you're interested in reading more about this). Taken together, this information means that autism spectrum disorders are all around you, and probably always have been.

Think about it this way—if you are in a school with 1,000 students, that means chances are there are probably 10 or more other kids right there in your school with a similar diagnosis. If you live in a town of 10,000 people, statistics say that 100 or more residents of your town will have such a disorder. Where are all of these people? If you can't immediately pick them out in a crowd, it may be because they have already developed strategies to help them manage everyday activities that are difficult for them.

This book was written to help you figure out some of these strategies. If you've ever played video games, then you know that you can get Official Strategy Guides for many of the most popular titles. Strategy guides tell you the rules of the game and give you special tips to be more successful on each of your missions. Think of this book as your own personal strategy guide for everyday life, with tips and tricks for the classroom and social situations, and for guiding you through behaviors and unwritten rules that you might not even have been aware of. All good strategy guides end with the achievement of an overall mission, and this book is no exception—we hope you can achieve your mission and take control of Asperger's syndrome or Nonverbal Learning Disorder.

Many of the examples presented in this book come directly from surveys of students diagnosed with AS or NLD. These are students just like you who have figured out some of the unwritten rules and have acquired strategies that they are eager to share. Other examples in this easy-to-use guide are composites or hypothetical situations based on the combined 20 years of experience of the authors. In all cases, names of students have been changed to protect privacy.

This book is divided into 10 chapters. The first two chapters will help you understand more about AS and NLD. Each of the remaining chapters will focus on an area where you may be having difficulty, and will include a summary of your mission and a list of tips and tricks to help you succeed. The last chapter is your Mission Log, where you can continue the quest on your own by identifying your own personal missions, the challenges you faced and the outcomes that resulted, and tips and tricks to remember for next time.

Using this strategy guide, you will learn the answers to the following questions:

➤ What are AS and NLD?
➤ How does having AS or NLD affect me?
➤ What is self-advocacy, and how can I practice it?
➤ What is assistive technology, and how can it help?
➤ How can I be successful with homework?
➤ How can I be successful in the classroom?
➤ What is the importance of good hygiene?
➤ How can I make and keep friends?
➤ How can I connect with other kids with AS and NLD?
➤ How can I continue to use these strategies to help me with future challenges?

Don't let the challenges of AS and NLD make parts of your day seem like you're in the middle of "mission impossible." Instead, we invite you to turn the page and learn strategies to help guide you through the rough patches and take control of challenging tasks, turning them into "mission accomplished."

CHAPTER 1

WHAT ARE ASPERGER'S SYNDROME AND NONVERBAL LEARNING DISORDER?

MISSION:

To learn about the strengths and challenges of having Asperger's syndrome or Nonverbal Learning Disorder.

t can be scary to hear someone tell you that you have a "syndrome" or a "disorder." What do those terms mean? Will it get better? You're going to learn the answers to both of these questions, and hopefully realize that having Asperger's syndrome (AS) or Nonverbal Learning Disorder (NLD) is not only nothing to be afraid of, but that when you're armed with the right knowledge and strategies, you can accomplish anything.

AS and NLD can be difficult to understand. Somebody with AS or NLD doesn't look any different from anyone else. People with AS or NLD can be just as smart as anyone else, too, or even smarter. The difference between **neurotypical** people, or those without any diagnosed disorders (NT's for short), and people with AS or NLD is in how you process information, interact with others, and see the world.

neurotypical: a way of referring to people who are not diagnosed with autism spectrum disorders

WHAT DOES IT MEAN?

Asperger's syndrome is an autism spectrum disorder, or part of a range of conditions that all include difficulties in the areas of communication and social skills, relationships with others, and certain restrictive or repetitive behaviors. Asperger's syndrome is considered to be on the high end of this range, meaning that people with this disorder can function pretty well despite these difficulties. Less is written about Nonverbal Learning Disorder, although some believe that it, too, may fall within the high end of the autism spectrum. Whether or not this turns out to be the case, there are many similarities between the two disorders and a few differences.

Neither one is an illness or a disease, but rather a neurological profile. Asperger's syndrome, named for researcher and doctor Hans Asperger, describes a specific pattern of observed behaviors. Nonverbal Learning Disorder is the name given to a learning profile characterized by a pattern of stronger skills in the areas traditionally associated with left-brain processing, and difficulties in areas commonly thought to be associated with right-brain processing. What this really means is that both AS and NLD are simply ways to describe the areas where, as a group, you differ from the way NT's think and behave.

Remember, neurotypical is an easier way to refer to people who haven't been diagnosed with any learning differences. Neurotypical doesn't mean "normal." The way you think and behave is normal for you; the way people without the diagnosis of AS or NLD react is normal for them.

DOES EVERYONE WITH ASPERGER'S SYNDROME OR NONVERBAL LEARNING DISORDER ACT THE SAME?

There is a wide variety in how having AS or NLD affects you. Two people with the same diagnosis can seem completely different. Why is this? AS and NLD are both names given to patterns of behavior and learning. These patterns consist of strengths in some areas, and weaknesses in others. Everyone with AS and NLD will have these strengths and weaknesses, but how strong the strong areas are, and how weak the weak areas are, can vary greatly. A good analogy is to think of a snowflake. In order to be a snowflake, each one must have six sides and be formed of ice, but within those parameters, each has different patterns so that no two look exactly alike.

As an example, when asked to define Asperger's syndrome in their own words, these high school students each focused on the aspects that affected them the most:

Sean, age 17: "It causes anxiety when in

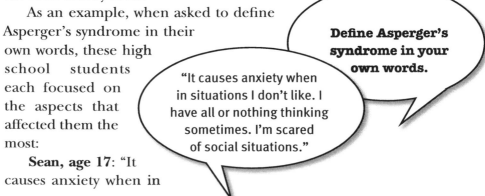

Define Asperger's syndrome in your own words.

"It causes anxiety when in situations I don't like. I have all or nothing thinking sometimes. I'm scared of social situations."

situations I don't like. I have all or nothing thinking sometimes. I'm scared of social situations."

Travis, age 16: "It's a big problem . . . nobody can understand, nor can they tell what the Asperger person is really feeling."

Bill, age 15: "Asperger's syndrome is a disability in which one lacks certain social awareness that's considered average by common standards. And an inability to express thoughts into words well."

In fact, difficulty understanding social situations, problems with appropriately expressing your feelings, and black and white thinking are all part of AS. Some of the other strengths and weaknesses that specialists look for when diagnosing AS are taken from a manual called the *Diagnostic and Statistical Manual of Mental Disorders* or **DSM-IV-TR** (it's the text revision of the fourth edition of this manual). This manual was published by the American Psychiatric Association in 2000, and lists criteria for professionals who make diagnoses. As listed in the DSM-IV, the criteria for diagnosing Asperger's syndrome include:

A.) Qualitative impairment in social interaction, as manifested by at least two of the following:

DSM-IV-TR: a manual published by the American Psychiatric Association that lists the criteria for diagnosing various disorders

(1) marked impairment in the use of multiple nonverbal behaviors such as eye-to-eye gaze, facial expression, body postures, and gestures to regulate social interaction

(2) failure to develop peer relationships appropriate to developmental level

(3) a lack of spontaneous seeking to share enjoyment, interests, or achievements with other people (e.g., by a lack of showing, bringing, or pointing out objects of interest to other people)

(4) lack of social or emotional reciprocity

B.) Restricted repetitive and stereotyped patterns of behavior, interests, and activities, as manifested by at
least one of the following:
  (1) encompassing preoccupation with one or more
  stereotyped and restricted patterns of interest
  that is abnormal either in intensity or focus
  (2) apparently inflexible adherence to specific, non-
  functional routines or rituals
  (3) stereotyped and repetitive motor mannerisms
  (e.g., hand or finger flapping or twisting, or complex whole-body movements)
  (4) persistent preoccupation with parts of objects
C.) The disturbance causes clinically significant impair-
ments in social, occupational, or other important
areas of functioning.
D.) There is no clinically significant general delay in language (e.g., single words used by age 2 years, commu-
nicative phrases used by age 3 years).
E.) There is no clinically significant general delay in cog-
nitive development or in the development of age-
appropriate self-help skills, adaptive behavior (other
than in social interaction) and curiosity about the environment in childhood. (p. 84)

That's a fairly dry, clinical look at the characteristics of Asperger's
syndrome. An easier way to interpret this information is to look at
some of these characteristics in terms of strengths and challenges.

Strengths:
➤ Average or above-average intelligence
➤ No delay in language development (meaning that you
began talking at the appropriate age)

Challenges:
➤ Having difficulty understanding and using body language
or maintaining eye contact
➤ Having difficulty developing and maintaining friendships
➤ Having difficulty understanding or empathizing with what
others might be feeling

➤ Having an intense interest in one or two specific topics or an intense focus on parts of objects to the extent that it interferes with other activities
➤ Having a hard time with changes in routine
➤ Engaging in repetitive movements, like hand flapping or spinning

All of these challenges can cause problems in social, occupational, or other important areas of life.

Nonverbal Learning Disorder, on the other hand, is diagnosed when there is a pattern of strengths and weaknesses demonstrating that the types of skills traditionally thought to be based in the right hemisphere, or half, of the brain are much weaker than those usually associated with the left hemisphere. Although current trends in brain research suggest that it may be more complicated than that, an important thing to note is that the areas of weakness found in NLD happen to coincide with many of the traits that make up Asperger's syndrome.

The name Nonverbal Learning Disorder can be misleading. At first you might think that "nonverbal" means people who don't talk. Actually, the opposite is true. People with NLD are very verbal, and usually have a good vocabulary and can have a very high reading level. Where they run into trouble, much like people with AS, is in interpreting social cues and body language—the *nonverbal* parts of communication. Students who have NLD describe it this way:

Adam, age 15: "Nonverbal Learning Disorder is different for everyone. It is a social and learning disorder."

Jason, age 16: "NLD means learning using primarily your hearing, not your sight."

Brian, age 10: "It means that one has trouble reading nonverbal body language signs such as anger, happiness or silliness. NLD isn't all doom and gloom however . . . there are areas where I excel. NLD is all about extremes."

Define Nonverbal Learning Disorder in your own words.

"It means that one has trouble reading nonverbal body language signs such as anger, happiness, or silliness. NLD isn't all doom and gloom however . . . there are areas where I excel. NLD is all about extremes."

Unlike Asperger's syndrome, Nonverbal Learning Disorder is not included in the DSM-IV-TR. Many professionals turn to the works of neuropsychologist Byron P. Rourke (1995) for a comprehensive explanation of the characteristics of Nonverbal Learning Disorder. The interesting thing about NLD is that professionals do, in fact, look for certain strengths, which they refer to as "neurological assets" to accompany specific areas of weakness, also referred to as "neurological deficits." There is no conclusive answer as to what causes the pattern of strengths and weaknesses of NLD. Rourke speculated that NLD might result from an irregularity of "white matter" in the brain, possibly having to do with damage to or dysfunction of the myelin sheaths, the insulating layer of fatty cells protecting the core of a nerve fiber. Margaret L. Bauman and Thomas L. Kemper later theorized in an article published in 2004 that the developing brain with autism may have multiple sites, such as the limbic system, hippocampus, brainstem, and cerebellum, that have differing types of abnormalities. However, they concluded that much more research is necessary before anything can be said for certain. One thing we do know for sure is, despite the fact that these syndromes have been given a name comparatively recently, AS and NLD have been around for a long time, and people have been successfully coping with these profiles for a long time. The particular dynamics and social demands of today's society have made these disorders more visible.

In the meantime, specialists continue to look for particular strengths and challenges when diagnosing NLD, and these are factors that you can understand and address. These include:

Strengths:
➤ Verbal abilities, sophisticated vocabulary
➤ Reading (decoding), although there may be difficulty in making inferences or predictions
➤ Spelling, although there are some exceptions

Challenges:
➤ Having difficulty understanding and using body language or maintaining eye contact
➤ Having difficulty developing and maintaining friendships
➤ Having a hard time with changes in routine

➤ Having difficulty with visual tasks (people with NLD learn better from hearing the information)

➤ Having difficulty with gross motor skills, meaning physical activities like throwing a ball or riding a bike

➤ Having difficulty with fine motor skills, meaning precise physical tasks like tying shoes, buttoning, or handwriting

➤ Having difficulties organizing, prioritizing, and monitoring or changing behavior (executive functioning skills)

WHAT ARE THE SIMILARITIES AND DIFFERENCES BETWEEN ASPERGER'S SYNDROME AND NONVERBAL LEARNING DISORDER?

Just looking at the lists above, you can probably start to see some traits between the two that are the same, such as difficulty in making and keeping friends, and understanding body language or maintaining eye contact. Even though some of the other traits listed under NLD are not part of the criteria for diagnosing AS, many of them also are found in people with AS. For instance, difficulty with gross and fine motor skills and executive functioning skills also are common with AS. Likewise, you will find some of the characteristics in the AS diagnosis to be common among people with NLD, especially black and white thinking. People with NLD also will sometimes show an intense interest in one or two topics, but usually to a lesser degree than people with AS, and usually not to the exclusion of everything else.

One of the major areas where AS and NLD differ is in the degree to which visual information processing is affected. To understand what visual information processing means, imagine that you come home from school and put your cell phone down on a messy desk. You turn around 5 minutes later and you just don't see it. You look everywhere, you rifle through your papers and the clutter, and it just doesn't seem to be there. You start to panic, and then you take another look, and there it is, sitting on top of your desk. You could have sworn it wasn't there a minute ago. The truth is it was there the whole time; it's just that with all the visual clutter you weren't able to zero in on it. We've all had this experience at one time or another. People with NLD perceive their world like this every day. It's as if their brain is assigning equal value to everything in their visual field, and nothing stands out like it should.

People with AS also can be affected by **visual information processing** issues, and can become overwhelmed in an area that is visually cluttered. However, despite this, many with AS are very good at visual tasks like reading a map, putting together puzzles, seeing patterns, and doing math. People with NLD perform poorly in these tasks, and do better when information is presented verbally; that is, talked out instead of demonstrated visually. It is the difference between thinking in images and thinking in words.

visual information processing: how your brain interprets what you see

The Venn diagram in Figure 1 illustrates where NLD and AS overlap, and the few areas in which they differ.

WILL MY ASPERGER'S SYNDROME OR NONVERBAL LEARNING DISORDER GO AWAY?

Asperger's syndrome or Nonverbal Learning Disorder explains some of how you learn and how you behave, but they don't define who you are as a person. People with AS and NLD possess both strengths and challenges. Of course, that can be said of just about anyone. Everyone has strengths, weaknesses, and particular characteristics that make up who they are. So it's not really a matter of AS or NLD going away, anymore than it would be a matter of, say, left-handedness going away. Just like lefties might need to use left-handed baseball gloves or scissors, there are strategies for people with AS and NLD that you can use to help you out when your way of thinking, perceiving, or reacting isn't working in a world that is set up a little bit differently.

Asperger's syndrome (AS)

Generally good at visual tasks; often visual thinkers

Repetitive behaviors

No delay in speech/language development

Intense interests or intense focus on parts of objects

Average to above-average intelligence

Both NLD and AS

Difficulty developing and maintaining friendships

Difficulty understanding and using body language

Difficulty maintaining eye contact

Gross and fine motor skills impairment

Black and white thinking

Hard time with changes in routine

Executive functioning issues/ difficulties with organizing, prioritizing, and monitoring/ changing behavior

Nonverbal Learning Disorder (NLD)

Difficulty with visual tasks; auditory processors

Can have delayed speech, sometimes due to delay in fine motor development

Intelligence can be any level

Figure 1. Comparison of NLD and AS.

Wrap Up: Things to Know About AS and NLD

➤ **Neither AS nor NLD is an illness or a disease.** They are simply behavioral and learning profiles that describe how you process information, interact with others, and see the world. Like everyone, people with AS and NLD possess both strengths and weaknesses.

➤ **AS is on the high-functioning end of the autism spectrum. Some believe that NLD also may be on the high end of the spectrum, but whether or not that turns out to be the case, NLD and AS have many things in common.** The autism spectrum is a range of conditions that all include difficulties in the areas of communication and social skills, relationships with others, and certain restrictive or repetitive behaviors.

➤ **No two people with AS or NLD are exactly alike.** Just like snowflakes all have six sides and are formed of ice crystals, yet all look different, everyone with AS or NLD will have a pattern of strengths in some areas and weaknesses in others, and what that looks like will differ from person to person.

➤ **People with AS or NLD share some similar characteristics**. These include challenges in the areas of: social skills; understanding and using body language; maintaining eye contact; gross and fine motor skills; black and white thinking; hard time with changes in routine; and a hard time with organizing, prioritizing, and monitoring/changing behavior (executive functioning skills).

➤ **There are some important differences between AS and NLD.** People with NLD learn better by hearing the information. People with AS are better at visual tasks.

➤ **AS or NLD will not go away, but having AS or NLD doesn't have to stand in your way.** Just like someone who is left-handed can play baseball with a lefty glove or cut more easily with left-handed scissors, you can accomplish challenging tasks by using helpful strategies.

CHAPTER 2

HOW DOES HAVING AS OR NLD AFFECT ME, AND HOW CAN THE STRATEGIES IN THIS BOOK HELP?

MISSION:

To understand how AS and NLD affect your everyday life.

Although the last chapter explained what AS and NLD are, the definitions don't tell the whole story. Definitions tend to focus mainly on the challenges faced by people with Asperger's syndrome or Nonverbal Learning Disorder, and often in a clinical, impersonal way. Along with the challenges of having AS or NLD, there also come strengths and positive attributes. Simply stated, when looking at the ways in which having AS or NLD affect you, there are some things that are good, and some that are not so good. This book will help you understand, through examples of others with AS and NLD, that you are not alone in the challenges you may be facing at home, in school, or among friends. The purpose of this book is to provide you with strategies that work to use your strengths to help overcome the challenges.

THE GOOD QUALITIES THAT COME WITH ASPERGER'S SYNDROME AND NONVERBAL LEARNING DISORDER

What can be good about having Asperger's syndrome or Nonverbal Learning Disorder? First, let's go right to the source. When asked what qualities they liked best about themselves, a group of students from across the country, all with AS or NLD, responded with similar traits:

Ryan, age 14: "I am trustworthy and honest."

Travis, age 16: "I am kind. I am persistent."

Steve, age 16: "My intelligence."

Mark, age 15: "I like that I keep my word."

Brian, age 10: "My power of conviction."

Bill, age 15: "My ability to use logic to make decisions more than the average person."

> What qualities do you like best about yourself?

> "My ability to use logic to make decisions more than the average person."

It should be no surprise to discover that these are some of the same characteristics that research scientists are identifying as strengths for people on the autism spectrum. For example, a 2008 study published in *Science Daily* showed that when the same choices were presented in different ways, one emphasizing the possible positive outcomes, and one emphasizing the possible negative outcomes, neurotypical people were influenced by how the information was presented to them. People with autism spectrum disorders, on the other hand, consistently made more rational decisions regardless of how the information was presented. This was attributed in part to their greater attention to details, and less reliance on emotion or instinct to make a decision.

Dr. Simon Baron-Cohen, a well-known expert on Asperger's syndrome, talked even further about the positive attributes of autism spectrum disorders in an interview with the BBC in January of 2009. He not only noted that people with autism possess special strengths and talents, but expressed his concern that if autism were ever eliminated, the world could lose out on the number of great mathematicians produced.

One company in Denmark actively seeks to recruit employees who have autism spectrum disorders. A *Wired* magazine article by Drake Bennet (2009) discussed Specialisterne, a successful IT consulting firm that primarily hires persons with autism. The company's founder, Thorkil Sonne, is the parent of a son with an autism spectrum disorder. He realized that people with these conditions pay greater attention to detail and excel at following routines, and were a natural match for a company responsible for finding software errors. The *Wired* article reported that similar companies are cropping up in other European countries.

It is worth noting that some of the greatest minds in history are now suspected to also have been people with AS or NLD, among them Albert Einstein, General George Patton, and Charles Darwin.

PROFILE: KATIE MILLER

Katie Miller is an award-winning artist who also happens to have a diagnosis of Asperger's syndrome. Katie was a recipient of the 2008 Wynn Newhouse Award for artists with disabilities, and has exhibited her paintings in numerous galleries and museums, including the Smithsonian Institution's S. Dillon Ripley Center in Washington, DC. Katie considers herself first and foremost an artist, but she also believes that being on the autism spectrum helps her to see the world differently and contributes to the persistence and creativity that has led to success in her field. She has a lot to say about the positive attributes of the autism spectrum, as well as how to deal with some of the challenges.

Did you always know that you had Asperger's syndrome?

I wasn't diagnosed until age 22, when I read about it on the Internet and my parents and I realized that this sounded just like me. Lots of girls get diagnosed later in life, because autism often presents itself differently in girls. For example, girls often have more "typical" intense interests than boys. If a boy is obsessed with vacuum cleaners, then it's pretty obvious. As a little girl, I was obsessed with baby dolls.

Lots of girls like to play with baby dolls, but each of my dolls had to have realistic attributes, and they all had birthdays and their own characteristics. I played with the other girls, but lost patience with them when they wanted to pretend things that babies couldn't really do. A girl would say, "Let's pretend she walked over here . . ." and I'd get really mad, because babies can't walk! I'd lose patience with girls who wouldn't support the baby doll's head like a real baby when they held it. I saved up my allowance to buy real baby clothes for the dolls. I had some friends, mostly girls who were more passive and went along with the way I wanted to play.

When did you become interested in art? What are some of the qualities that you attribute to autism that you feel have helped you succeed?

My whole life I've been interested in art. One of my earliest memories is watching Bob Ross [host of "The Joy of Painting," a long-running series on PBS] on TV. I loved colors and drawing. As a kid, I was not a savant, I just had a very intense interest. But the older I got, the better I got because I spent so much time drawing.

At about age 5, I decided I wanted to be an artist. I carried a sketchbook everywhere I went, and I refused to go with my parents to restaurants with dim lighting, because I couldn't draw. My style was very realistic. By age 14, I was getting portrait commissions.

At about 14 ½ or 15, a high school art teacher turned me on to the idea that art wasn't just about copying pictures, but could express thoughts and ideas. I never realized this before. I was really amazed, because I had all these creative ideas and now I had a way to express them. So that's when I stopped copying other pictures. But as a child, I was so intent on copying pictures, it gave me a skill set that others didn't have. I also find that while my heightened sensory perception can be disabling in some aspects, my sensitivity to color, shape, line, and detail really helps my art. I notice things other people don't.

So art was always an area of strength and interest. Did you have any challenges in school?

I always got good grades in school, but I often got by with memorizing, especially in math. I never understood the concepts, and the teachers didn't, either, or at least they didn't know how to explain it to me in a way that made sense. Like imaginary numbers—to me, an imaginary number was 13 unicorns plus 5 leprechauns. And the teachers couldn't explain why that wasn't an imaginary number. So I just accepted that I didn't really understand math, but I could memorize the answers and get A's.

Were there any challenges that stand out in your mind that you had to overcome to achieve the success that you now have? How did you meet those challenges?

I studied art in Italy for one and a half months when I was in college. I wasn't sure how I'd be able to last, because I don't deal well with big changes. I had been to Europe on vacation with my parents before, but this was very different. I almost went home several times, but I'm so proud I stuck it out, and I loved it even though I had a really hard time.

I had discovered AS on the Internet just prior to the trip, and we had an appointment with a neuropsychologist for when I got back, but I didn't feel right saying I had Asperger's because it wasn't an official diagnosis yet. I had to just explain to people the things I had difficulty with.

I have major issues with food due to sensitivities with taste and texture. I had packed a big box with boxes of macaroni and cheese, protein bars that I like, and other nonperishables and sent it ahead. The school thought the box had arrived, but it didn't. So I had no food for the whole first week. I had to be driven into town to pick out things I would eat from the little grocery store. And there was this nice Italian grandma type who was cooking for the students. Everyone raved about her cooking, but I couldn't eat any of it. People wondered why, and so I explained that I had heightened sensitivities. I told them that I heard things other people didn't hear, saw things other people couldn't, and taste was very intense to me. They said, "Wow, you're like a superhero!" I laughed and said, "Yeah, but it's not really that fun." But I thought it was cool that they were curious and supportive of my differences, even though at that time I couldn't put a name to it.

Do you have any tips from your experience to help other students with AS or NLD?

If you just tell people what you are having trouble with and what you need, they'll usually want to help you. Eventually people will sense that you're different, and if they don't know why they're more hesitant with you. If they can put a name to it, they are more accepting. Nobody wants to make fun of the disabled, but they will make fun of people who are just weird.

CHALLENGES OF LIVING WITH AS AND NLD

As you have seen, there also are a number of challenges that result from having AS or NLD. These challenges can affect many areas of your life, including school, home, and friendships. You may recognize yourself in some of the areas of difficulty outlined below. If you do, you're not alone. The same group of students with AS and NLD who identified their good qualities also listed the things they found most difficult to do. Their lists included:

Travis, age 16: "Socializing; managing my temper."

Sean, age 17: "Making new friends, being in crowds."

Bill, age 15: "Organization."

Alex, age 14: "Having lots of homework, writing, running."

Steve, age 16: "Complex math."

Mark, age 15: "Cleaning up after myself."

List the things you find most difficult to do.

"Making new friends, being in crowds."

All of these challenges correspond with the difficulties commonly identified in research and literature as being associated with AS and NLD. Some of them, like math, tend to pose more of a challenge for those with NLD than those with AS. They can be grouped into broader categories, explained briefly below. Each of these issues also will be addressed in the remainder of the book, and will be identified as your "mission." To help accomplish your mission and take control of your disorder, you will receive strategies, or tips and tricks to help you achieve success in tasks and everyday activities where you might feel like you are struggling.

SOCIAL SKILLS

Social skills refer to how effectively you interact with other people. Among the items in the students' list above, the category of social skills includes "socializing" and "making new friends," and also can be a factor in why you might have difficulty "being in a crowd."

Conversation and communication are important parts of good social skills. Although people with AS or NLD generally have pretty sophisticated vocabularies, and children with these diagnoses are sometimes referred to as "little professors," communication is more than just words. Studies show that as much as 93% of communication takes place on a nonverbal level. How can this be, when conversation, by definition, means speaking? What it means is that even when someone is speaking to you, the meaning of his words can be changed by the tone of his voice and his facial expressions, gestures, and other body posturing. As a group, people with AS or NLD have a lot of difficulty naturally reading this body language. If you are concentrating only on the words, you are missing out on an important part of the conversation. You might even end up misinterpreting the intent behind the words.

At the same time, people with AS or NLD can be pretty talkative. You may struggle, however, with language **pragmatics**, or the conversational give and take that comes more naturally to neurotypical folks. You will recall that part of the definition of AS includes an intense interest in a particular subject or activity, almost to the exclusion of other interests. This can mean

pragmatics: using language appropriate to social situations; knowing what to say, how to say it, and when to say it

that someone with AS may keep talking about her favorite subject long after her friends have lost interest in the conversation.

To complicate matters, consider this: How do you tell when someone has lost interest in a conversation? A neurotypical person may indicate that he is ready to move on with a variety of nonverbal signals, such as looking away, rolling his eyes, crossing his arms over his chest, or shifting his feet uncomfortably. All of these cues are considered by neurotypicals to be polite ways of hinting, and all of these hints will be lost on you if you are not paying attention to body language.

At the same time, because you might be relying on words, you might indicate your boredom verbally. Have you ever ended a conversation by saying, "I'm finished talking about that now," or, "I don't care about that"? You may not realize that these statements are considered rude by NT listeners, even though they actually may be trying to convey the same message nonverbally.

Chapters 8 and 9 can help you in these areas. Your mission in Chapter 8 will be to understand friendship. Your mission in Chapter 9 will be making connections to meet new friends. Both chapters include stories from students with AS and NLD who have had problems understanding friendship and meeting new friends, and will give you strategies to use your areas of interest to help develop your social skills.

EXECUTIVE FUNCTIONING SKILLS

When people talk about problems with "organization" and "having lots of homework," as the students who we surveyed did, they are really talking about executive functioning skills. Have you ever gotten up late for school thinking: "Did I do my homework?" "Do I have a test today?" or "Where did I put my backpack?" These are common questions asked by students with AS or NLD, as well as neurotypical students. They are all related to executive functioning deficits, which means difficulty with:

➤ selecting appropriate goals;
➤ getting started on your work;
➤ knowing which assignment or activity to do first, or prioritizing;
➤ organizing your thoughts and materials; and

➤ understanding what you are doing at that moment in time.

Fortunately, there are both strategies and assistive technologies available to help manage some of the confusion that comes with executive functioning deficits. Chapter 4 will help you understand how technology can help. Your mission in Chapter 5 will be to discover strategies to succeed with homework. Both chapters will have lots of tips for organizational skills.

INFORMATION PROCESSING

In the last chapter you learned that having AS or NLD means that you process information differently than neurotypical people do. As an adult, this may actually become an advantage. Just like Katie Miller, and like Albert Einstein, Charles Darwin, and General Patton, you may have ways of seeing, interpreting, or analyzing things that don't occur to other people. It means that in some areas you can excel.

Unfortunately, as a student, differences in information processing can cause problems in school, including the problems in writing and math from the students' list above. Information may not be presented in a way that makes sense to you. Additionally, slow processing can make you feel like others are racing ahead of you with the answers while you are still thinking about the question.

When Max, an elementary school student, was diagnosed with Nonverbal Learning Disorder, he learned that the reason why some things that seemed easy to the rest of the class were difficult for him was because his brain processed information differently from most of his classmates. He also realized that he somehow knew this all along. As Max described:

Sometimes in school, the teacher calls on me, and I know that I know the answer, but I just can't get it out. And I imagine that inside my brain there's a computer with a CD-ROM. And there are all these little mice running around and feeding CDs into the computer. But it's like they can't find the right CD fast enough.

Except for the part about the mice, Max's self-assessment is fairly on target. The answers are there in his brain, it just takes a little longer for him to retrieve them than it does for his classmates.

Strategies to help you succeed in the classroom and to work around information processing issues are presented in Chapter 6, where your mission will be classroom success.

MOTOR AND SENSORY-BASED SKILLS

Do you hate P.E. class? Gross motor skills, or physical activities like throwing a ball or riding a bike, are identified as an area of weakness in people with NLD, and often are an area of difficulty in those with Asperger's syndrome as well. In fact, looking at the list compiled by students with AS and NLD, you can see that along with academic and social challenges, "running" is another area that was identified as something that is difficult to do. Team sports and other activities in P.E. class can be a real challenge, not only because you might be perceived as clumsier than your friends, but because the difficulties you also may have with information processing can mean that you need a little longer to react to fast-paced team activities. Maybe you already work with an occupational therapist to help you in these areas. If you are still struggling, Chapter 9, where your mission is making connections and meeting new friends, also offers some suggestions for healthy fitness activities that are not team-based.

Fine motor skills, or precise physical tasks like tying shoes, buttoning, or even handwriting, pose another common challenge for those with AS or NLD. This can be one of the reasons why "cleaning up after myself" also made the list of difficult things to do. When talking about a messy room, executive functioning and organizational skills may hamper your ability to keep everything straight. However, when referring to hygiene, sometimes difficulty with fine motor skills or sensory-based issues may be interfering with your ability to keep yourself neat and clean.

Sensory-based issues mean that you may be especially sensitive to smell, taste, touch or texture, or even sights and sounds, and find things offensive or unpleasant that other people hardly seem to notice. Sensitivity to tags on clothing, for instance, could make certain shirts very uncomfortable for you to wear. It is worth mentioning that along with the sensations that affect your body, sensory issues can mean that you also are more affected by sounds, bright lights, or visual clutter. Along with the social skills challenges of being in a crowd, sensory issues also can make being around crowds of people unpleasant for you. Chapter 7, where your mission is to develop good hygiene, will help you with strategies to work around the challenges in maintaining appearance and good hygiene presented by fine motor skills and sensory-based issues.

ANXIETY AND STRESS

Anxiety, meltdowns, and shut-downs are probably the most all-encompassing difficulties faced by kids with AS and NLD. When you are overwhelmed with worry and confusion, and don't yet have the problem-solving skills to deal with a stressful situation, the two most common ways to react are to shut down or to melt down. This also can explain why "managing my temper" was an important item on the students' list.

What can cause this level of anxiety? You don't need to look any further than the challenges described above. Imagine a situation where you aren't understanding social cues so you're not really sure how to react, and add to that some tasks you need to accomplish in the classroom that might be made a little more confusing because of challenges with organizational skills and information processing, factor in some sensory issues, such as the student next to you tapping a pencil, which most of the class doesn't seem to notice but sounds like a drum to you, and suddenly, it's time to turn in your essay and you've barely even begun . . . wow! That's a lot of stuff to have to deal with at once.

Some people react by shutting down. You become so overwhelmed or confused by the situation around you, whether it is facing a mountain of homework at home, being in a noisy crowd of kids on the playground, or not understanding how to start an assignment in class, that you just stop. Some kids call it "zoning out." Teachers or adults who don't understand might think you're just not paying attention. But there's much more to it than that. Maybe this scenario seems familiar:

"I can't believe I failed another test!" Jack said as he walked through his door after school. He had studied all night and was sure he had everything down perfectly. Then the quiz was in front of him, with the essay form, and he panicked. All of the other kids were writing furiously and he just sat there, staring at a blank paper, thinking, "What's the point? I can't write, so why bother?" Jack thought about his teacher, Mr. B., coming over to him and not saying a word. "Mr. B could care less that I didn't know how to start the essay," Jack yelled to no one in particular. "Why should he? I'm just another kid who learns differently. It's not fair that everything is so hard for me."

Experiences like Jack's are not unique. He gave up before he started. He felt completely in over his head, and couldn't even think about what else to do.

Sometimes instead of shutting down, you find yourself becoming more and more angry. The anxiety, confusion, and emotions can be so overwhelming that you find yourself in a full-blown temper tantrum or meltdown, even if you didn't mean to lose control. You might feel awful afterward, but at the time, you just couldn't help it. And even though you really want to be able to keep it together next time, you don't know how you are going to manage.

What can you do about shutdowns and meltdowns? You probably already know that in the moment, it's really hard to snap out of it. One trick is to think of strategies in advance to give you options in situations that can quickly become overwhelming. Imagine what Jack's day could have been like if he already knew a few tips and tricks to help him start his essay? Or imagine that instead of getting angry with kids on the playground who don't want to play the games you like, you had a list of things you could say to help them understand how you felt.

One of the most important things to realize is that you are your own best advocate. You are in charge of yourself. Your first mission in this book, in the very next chapter, will be to be able to explain your needs and not be afraid to ask for help. This also is known as self-advocacy.

A WORD ABOUT BLACK AND WHITE THINKING

Fifteen-year-old Bill, a high school student with Asperger's syndrome, was asked to think about some of his best qualities. He described one of his personal areas of strength as, "Not letting views of others change or distort my own." Although persistence and the ability to make logic-based decisions despite the opinions of others certainly are positive attributes, there is a danger that you may become so entrenched in your views that you aren't even open to any other possibilities. This is part of the black and white thinking aspect of AS and NLD. Something is either right, or it's wrong.

This is where this strategy guide will challenge you the most. Most strategies are built on the premise that there are more options than all or nothing, yes or no, right or wrong. If you can allow yourself to open up your mind to other possibilities, suddenly you'll find that you have many more choices than you thought. So with that in mind, are you ready to embark on your mission? Believe it or not, you already have what it takes to succeed!

Wrap Up: What's Good and What's Not So Good About AS and NLD?

➤ **There are strengths and positive attributes that come with having AS or NLD.** Students with AS and NLD were able to identify a number of positive traits when surveyed, and many of these have even been backed up with scientific research. The students identified the following good qualities associated with AS or NLD: being trustworthy, honest, kind, and intelligent; keeping one's word; and having persistence, power of conviction, and an ability to use logic to make decisions more than the average person.

➤ **Some very famous and creative people are now thought to have had Asperger's syndrome or Nonverbal Learning Disability, including Albert Einstein, General George Patton, and Charles Darwin.** Current high achievers with autism spectrum disorders, such as award-winning artist Katie Miller, attribute some of their success to the strengths that come with autism spectrum disorders.

➤ **There also are a number of challenges connected with these disorders.** The same students who identified their areas of strength considered the following to be their main areas of difficulty: socializing, making new friends, being in crowds, organizing, having lots of homework, writing, doing math, running, cleaning up after one's self, and managing one's temper.

➤ **This strategy guide will help you find ways to use your areas of strength to help with the things that are challenging.** It will provide advice and tips from students with AS and NLD in the areas of self-advocacy, social skills, executive functioning skills, information processing, motor and sensory issues, and black and white thinking. Being able to plan out strategies in advance can help alleviate stress before challenges become too overwhelming and result in a shutdown or meltdown.

➤ **Despite some challenges related to AS and NLD that can affect home life, school, and friendships, you have what it takes to succeed!** You can learn to use the skills you are very good at to help you out in the areas that are more difficult for you.

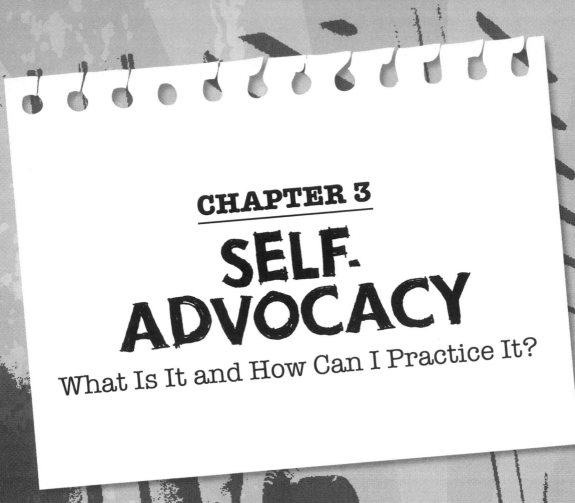

CHAPTER 3
SELF-ADVOCACY
What Is It and How Can I Practice It?

MISSION:
To be able to explain your needs and not be afraid to ask for help.

ALAN'S EYES

Alan is a fifth-grade student who was diagnosed with Nonverbal Learning Disorder (NLD). Like most people with AS or NLD, Alan finds maintaining eye contact very difficult, sometimes impossible. Students with AS or NLD have even gone so far as to say that trying to remember to look people in the eye while speaking can be so distracting to them that it interferes with their ability to concentrate on what is actually being said. So when Alan's teacher asked the class to share examples of how to show respect to one another, and a student volunteered, "We show respect by looking at other people when they talk," Alan knew that he had to set the record straight. He didn't want his classmates to think he was rude. When the teacher called on him, Alan said, "There's something that you should know. It really almost hurts me to look other people in the eye because I have NLD. You should remember that I'm still listening, even if I'm not looking at you." His teacher thanked Alan, and Alan later told his mother that the students in the classroom were very receptive and understanding.

Alan demonstrated self-advocacy when he explained to his classmates why he didn't look them in the eye so that they wouldn't misinterpret his actions.

WHAT IS SELF-ADVOCACY?

Advocacy is defined as an individual's ability to effectively communicate, convey, negotiate, or assert his or her own interests, desires, needs, and rights. It involves making informed decisions and taking responsibility for those decisions (Van Reusen & Bos, 1994). Self-advocacy means making those around you aware of your needs, just as Alan did, so that they will understand or support you.

> **advocacy:** an individual's ability to effectively communicate, convey, negotiate, or assert his or her own interests, desires, needs, and rights

For a person with AS or NLD, who often thinks or behaves differently than a neurotypical person might expect, self-advocacy is a very powerful tool. Asking for help when you need it is one part of self-advocacy. You also need to be able to explain why you do what you do, and why it's OK, especially when you might be acting differently from your peers. Self-advocacy is a way to turn a seemingly odd behavior into just another logical aspect of being you.

Theresa, a young woman who is now in her 20s, provides another example of good self-advocacy.

THERESA'S SPINNING

For as long as she can remember, Theresa has engaged in "stimming," or repetitive behaviors that may seem unusual to outsiders, but help her to calm herself in overwhelming situations and environments. Theresa has given a lot of thought to what drives these repetitive behaviors, and why they are important to her. She explains:

"I have always paced/galloped around my room and talked to myself, since I was 2. Mom calls it 'dancing,' because it usually is to music. She admits it looks funny, but thinks it is because I can't dance. She may be right. Spinning, pacing, and jumping up and down are perfect ways to move without crossing your midline, which has never been my thing.

"When I was little, I was small enough to gallop across the room and bounce off the walls with my hands. But now that I'm bigger and live on someone's ceiling, that doesn't work . . . especially when you factor in the shouting of random words. So I took up rocking and hand-flapping as a neighborly courtesy. I actually spent time thinking about how to solve this problem, and would not have thought of this solution had I not read books by people with autism.

"But I definitely NEED time to do this, every day. I don't have a definitive answer on why I do this, but I'll try to put it into words. I am overwhelmed by huge environments and lots of visual clutter. At times like this I go into 'zombie mode,' which keeps me from freaking out. At recess, when lots of kids were running around and I couldn't find where my friends were, I'd find a huge empty space and spin in circles until the outside world really *wasn't* there. Also, it could be some sensory idiosyncrasy, and violent, repetitive movement just feels good to me. I love amusement park rides, too."

Theresa was self-aware enough not only to be able to explain why this unusual behavior was important to her, but as she matured she also was able to moderate her behaviors so that they fulfilled her needs without unnecessarily disturbing others.

SELF-ADVOCACY IN SCHOOL

You will find that self-advocacy, or strategies to help people understand your needs, will play an important part in almost every aspect of your daily life, whether it is at home, at school, or among friends. Alan and Theresa used self-advocacy to explain behaviors that seemed out of the ordinary to friends and classmates. Once their friends understood, these behaviors became more socially acceptable. Additional self-advocacy strategies can be found throughout this book. In the meantime, here is a brief overview of some of the ways in which you can advocate for yourself.

Self-advocacy is an excellent way to counter unrealistic expectations. As you've seen in the last chapter, people with AS and NLD possess many strengths and talents. Because there are many things that you can do well, teachers, friends, and even family members may not completely understand why some things are difficult for you, or why you aren't reacting the way they would expect.

Being able to explain to somebody why you are confused, stressed, or uncomfortable and how they can help may go a long way toward making that situation better. You might be afraid that if you ask for help or clarification you will appear "stupid." Nothing could be farther from the truth. Any teacher will tell you that there are no stupid questions, but you may present the wrong impression if you say nothing. Then people around you will assume that you know what is going on. When it turns out that you don't, they often will jump to the wrong conclusion—that you aren't paying attention, or that you are "choosing" not to work. They get angry, you get angry and defensive, and things can spiral downward from there.

A group of eight students diagnosed with AS or NLD were asked the question, "What might you say to a teacher or an adult when you don't understand something?" Most of their responses were similar:

Steve, age 16: "Excuse me, can you please explain that to me one more time?"

Sean, age 17: "I need help."

Brian, age 10: "Can you please help me understand this?"

In fact, seven out of eight responded with statements such as, "I need help," or, "Could you explain that again?" When asked what they might say to a friend or classmate, the answers were a little less formal:

Sean, age 17: "I'm confused."

Steve, age 16: "Hey, can you help me with this?"

Brian, age 10: "Hey, can you help me understand this because I'm very confused."

> "What might you say to a teacher or an adult when you don't understand something?"

> "Excuse me, can you please explain that to me one more time?"

One student, however, had a very different response. When asked what he might say to a teacher or an adult when he didn't understand something, Mark would rather not admit that he was confused.

Mark, age 15: "I would tell the teacher I'm not doing this."

Can you see where a response like this might create a problem? What might the teacher think?

> ➤ The teacher might think that the student was refusing to do his work without any apparent reason. This would probably make the teacher angry and lead to a confrontation.

> ➤ The teacher might think that the student was challenging his or her authority. A situation like his could also escalate, resulting in a failing grade or even a trip to the principal's office.

What might be a better strategy? Rather than saying, "I'm not doing this," the student could explain, "I can't do this because . . ." and tell the teacher what it was that he found confusing. If he wasn't able to put that into words, he could also say, "I'm so confused about this that I don't think I can do it." Now how might the teacher react?

➤ The teacher would know that the student wasn't starting his work because there was something he didn't understand.

➤ Instead of getting angry, the teacher would offer to help.

Don't be afraid to ask for help. It's not only a better strategy than the alternative, but it's also your right.

IEPS AND 504 PLANS

Did you know that as a student with a disability that impacts your education (or makes it so that you are unable to do some of the things your classmates can do in the same way that they do it) you may be entitled by law to certain rights? Students with disabilities who need special education and related services are guaranteed the right to a free appropriate public education (also known as FAPE) under the Individuals with Disabilities Education Act (IDEA) of 2004. This includes specialized instruction and/or modifications to the learning program to meet your needs. Students with disabilities also have the right to accommodations in the educational program so that they are not unfairly discriminated against because of their disability under Section 504 of the Rehabilitation Act of 1973.

What are classroom accommodations? **Accommodations** are changes to the way your teacher presents information, or to the way you are required to complete assignments or take tests, based on your needs. Common accommodations include extra time to complete assignments or take tests or priority seating so that you are less distracted. Accommodations also can include things like receiving copies of notes if your

accommodations: changes to the way your teacher presents information, or to the way you are required to complete assignments or take tests, based on your needs

handwriting or information processing issues interfere with your ability to take notes while listening to instruction.

As a minor, you will need to enlist the help and support of your parent or guardian to follow the paths laid out by these laws to secure an **Individualized Education Program (IEP)** or a **504 Plan**. If you are struggling in school due to your disabilities and you don't have these, here is your first opportunity for self-advocacy:

> **Individualized Education Program (IEP) or 504 Plan:** documents that explain your strengths and needs as a student with AS or NLD and make plans for how your teachers and other school personnel can help you succeed

> ➤ Tell your parents or guardian that the diagnosis of your disability, along with the difficulties that you are having in school, may entitle you to an IEP or 504 Plan. With an IEP or 504 Plan, your parents can work with your public school to get you extra support in your areas of need.
> ➤ Private schools are a whole different story, and may or may not be covered under these laws depending on whether they receive public funding. However, even if you are a student in a private school, you are entitled to a free evaluation by your public school district. Your public school district may develop strategies to share with your private school.
> ➤ Direct your parents/guardian to see the Resources section at the back of this book for recommendations for additional reading on advocacy for students with special needs.

Maybe you already have an IEP or 504 Plan in place. If so, do you know what's on it?

> ➤ Be aware of what is on your plan. If you don't know, ask your parents, guardian, or teacher/special educator to review it with you.
> ➤ Keep a list of your accommodations taped to the inside cover of your notebook, so that you can refer back to it.

There may be times when knowing this information can make your day a lot easier. For instance, Ryan, a middle school student with Nonverbal Learning Disorder, knew that his IEP allowed him to use a calculator in math class even during times when other students normally wouldn't be using one. This was never a problem, until one day he walked into class and there was a substitute teacher. The substitute passed out a worksheet, and told the class, "No calculators for this assignment." Ryan didn't panic. He quietly went over to the substitute teacher and said, "Excuse me, but I have an IEP and I'm allowed to use a calculator for classroom assignments." The substitute teacher then let him use his calculator.

If Ryan had not advocated for himself, this situation could have ended very badly. Maybe he wouldn't have been able to keep up and complete the assignment in time. Maybe he would have shut down, so overwhelmed at the amount of work and no calculator that he couldn't even bring himself to start. Maybe he would have even gotten in trouble, because the substitute wouldn't understand why he wasn't following directions. None of these things happened because Ryan knew what he was entitled to, and spoke up.

If you already have an IEP or 504 Plan, did you know that your teacher, your parents, and other members of the school team will meet at least once a year to discuss your progress and decide what you need for the next year? You can, and should, play an active role in this process.

➤ If you are not already attending your IEP Annual Review meetings, or 504 Plan meetings, ask your parents, guardian, or teacher to include you.

➤ If you are in elementary or middle school, it may or may not be appropriate for you sit through the entire meeting, which can be quite long and formal. Instead, you can be given the opportunity to come to the meeting for the last 15 minutes or so, and have the team explain to you what your goals and/or accommodations will be, and ask for your thoughts and ideas.

➤ If you are in high school, it is a good idea to be an active participant in all parts of the meeting, to give you practice for when you need to advocate for yourself as an adult.

How do you self-advocate in a situation that isn't covered by an IEP or 504 Plan, but where you need a teacher to understand your point of view?

> ➤ Talk to your teacher. He or she may not be available right at that moment, but maybe you can schedule some time to see your teacher privately during lunch or before or after school.

> ➤ If you are afraid to approach your teacher or don't know what to say, you can practice with another adult. Your guidance counselor or your parents or guardian can help you figure out what to say.

> ➤ Use specific examples wherever possible. Telling your teacher, "Math is hard," is not as helpful as explaining, "I'm having trouble lining up the numbers when I do long division and that's getting me confused."

> ➤ Make a list of the things you want to talk about, so that you can refer back to it during your conversation. You also can make a list after you work out some strategies, so that you can reflect back on what options you came up with.

SELF-ADVOCACY AND BULLYING

Although many schools strive for "zero tolerance" when it comes to bullying, somehow the bullies still seem to find a way to single out kids who are different. Self-advocacy is an important weapon in your arsenal to combat bullying. Bullies look for easy opportunities and for kids who will have a strong reaction. They also look for kids who they can intimidate into not telling an adult. Sometimes it is hard to figure out whether someone is teasing you in a friendly way, or being a bully. It can be even harder to know what to do about it.

FRIENDLY TEASING OR BULLYING?

Once you start getting a little older, especially in middle school, you'll find that friends begin to tease each other. They might say something that sounds awful, but mean it as a joke.

How can you tell if someone is engaging in friendly teasing or bullying? Here are some questions to ask yourself:

➤ Is this person usually nice to you, or does he only tease you?

➤ Does he talk to everyone this way, or does he seem to be singling you out?

➤ Do you ever tease back? How does this person react if you do?

➤ If you tell this person that he hurt your feelings, does he apologize? Or does he continue to make fun of you?

➤ If an adult or another friend accuses this person of acting mean toward you, does he then try to blame you for his actions?

If the answers to most of these questions fall on the side of someone who is usually nice to you, and genuinely seems to feel bad if your feelings have been hurt, chances are this is friendly teasing. If, on the other hand, this is someone who only teases you, gets angry if you tease back, continues to engage in behavior that he knows upsets you, or blames the way you act for the fact that he's teasing you, this is no friend. You will be better off avoiding him, or if the situation escalates, using proactive and reactive self-advocacy strategies to bring it to an end.

PROACTIVE STRATEGIES: SEEK OUT SUPPORT DURING UNSTRUCTURED TIMES

There are some proactive strategies you can use to avoid placing yourself in situations where you might be bullied. Being **proactive** means taking action before there is a problem.

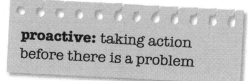

proactive: taking action before there is a problem

The easiest time for a bully to pick on another student is when there are no teachers or adults around to catch him or her. That is why lunchtime, recess, and the school bus are prime examples of when bullying might take place. The advice most often given by adults is to surround yourself with a group of friends, so that bullies will be hesitant to approach you. So what happens if you don't have a large group of friends? What if you prefer to eat lunch alone?

Be aware of whether or not an area is supervised by adults.

Ryan, the same middle school student who advocated successfully for his calculator in math class, was faced with this challenge in the noisy, chaotic middle school cafeteria. His solution was to choose a seat at the table near the door. Why? Because Ryan observed that the teachers tended to congregate there during their lunch duty. As Ryan put it, "It was the most watched table in the whole cafeteria!" He knew there was no chance for anybody to get away with anything while there were a bunch of teachers standing close by. Other students have solved this problem by asking a teacher if they could eat lunch in her classroom instead of in the cafeteria.

Look for other options besides the playground during recess.

Recess can pose special challenges, especially if kids are running all over the playground without adequate adult supervision. You can practice your self-advocacy skills by asking an adult to help take charge of a structured game during recess. You also can ask if it's possible to go to a quieter area, like the media center.

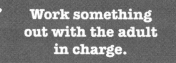

Work something out with the adult in charge.

Self-advocacy was a strategy that worked well for Brian, an elementary school student who was being harassed by kids on the school bus. When some of the older kids started regularly teasing Brian in the back of the bus, Brian found some time to talk to the bus driver and tell him what was going on. The bus driver suggested that Brian sit up front, right behind him. Brian took his advice, and the older kids left him alone once he switched his seat.

These are all ways to avoid places and activities that might become opportunities for bullying. What can you do if you are already being bullied? How can self-advocacy change the situation?

REACTIVE STRATEGIES: WHEN AND HOW TO SPEAK UP

Bullies feel empowered, or stronger, when they know there are no adults around to catch them. Bullies also may feel empowered when they believe that no matter what they do, you won't tell on them. They may tell you, "Nobody likes a tattletale." They may even threaten to hurt you if you tell an adult.

It's important to recognize that someone who is targeting you, whether it is by saying mean things or by being physically aggressive and hurting you, is not your friend. Not telling on him or her isn't going to make the person like you more. And it's especially important to tell an adult if you are being hurt or threatened. Remember that it is the bully who is in the wrong, not you. If you don't say anything, it's only going to give the bully confidence that he or she can get away with more. At the same time, yelling back or making threats yourself will most likely escalate the situation, or make it worse. Reactive strategies are just what they sound like—ways to react in the moment and speak up.

How do you speak up about bullying? There are a few ways to do this.

Address the bully directly. This takes courage, and may or may not be effective. Speaking up to a bully can mean saying something as honest as, "I don't think that's funny," or, "Stop it." A bully is looking to provoke a strong reaction from you. Stating your feelings calmly can sometimes take the "fun" out of bullying and put a stop to the situation.

Use a "comeback" line, or turn something that was said to be mean into a joke. Humor often can diffuse a tense situation, but there are advantages and disadvantages to this approach. Ryan's favorite comeback line was, "I know you are, but what am I?" The first few times he used this, it got a laugh. After awhile, Ryan found that this didn't always work. It's hard to think fast in the moment, and even harder to come up with something funny and appropriate to say. Eventually, Ryan's standard comeback line became predictable, and was another source of teasing. Bear in mind that the best comeback lines often are spontaneous.

Tell an adult. Speaking up to an adult usually is the most effective way to begin to defend yourself against bullying. A school guidance counselor can be a good resource, and so can your parents or guardians. You can do this in private, on your own time, without announcing, "I'm telling."

Problem solving with a trusted adult often is the beginning step to making the situation better. In order to make this happen, you will need to be able to calmly explain what happened, make the adult aware of your needs, and ask for help in dealing with the situation. Sound familiar? This also is the definition of self-advocacy.

SELF-ADVOCACY AT HOME

Self-advocacy at home requires a different skill set. You are in your comfort zone, and your family is already aware of your disability and how it affects your lives. This feeling of safety can promote your self-advocacy skills. Here is the cool part: You may not even realize it, but your family or support system at home can help you practice self-advocacy skills.

For example, if your parents expect you to make your bed before leaving for school, and you feel like you just can't do one more thing in the morning, what are your options? You can:

➤ Get into a shouting match with your parents.
➤ Leave without making your bed.
➤ Force yourself to make your bed, and become very agitated in the process.
➤ Explain to your parents that your morning is very busy, and you don't feel like you can fit in extra time to make your bed. Be prepared to negotiate other options. For example, maybe you can straighten out your bed when you come home from school.

Hopefully you can easily see that the last option gives you the best chance of resolving the situation without creating more stress and tension.

An essential step in advocating for yourself is to take some time to think before reacting. It is hard to calmly advocate for yourself in the middle of a conflict. It's OK to ask your parents if you can have a little bit of time to think about the situation. It also might be a good idea to talk to your parents at a time when everything is calm and quiet, and work out a strategy with them so that they remember that you need your think time.

Another common area where you can practice self-advocacy at home is with the issue of homework. In Chapter 5, you will learn many strategies for managing your homework. In the meantime, it is important to be able to use self-advocacy to explain your needs. For example, you may feel that it is unfair that your family makes you finish your homework before watching TV, when your homework takes up so much time that you sometimes don't even get any television time. You have at least three options. You could:

1. Yell at your parents.
2. Watch television anyway.
3. Explain to your parents that you are upset because you have so much homework to do that you won't have enough time to finish it, plus watch television.

Which one would you choose? Number one is an impulsive reaction, but normal. Number two is defiant and will only get you in more trouble. Number three is self-advocating. You are expressing your feelings in an appropriate manner and then giving them a concrete reason why you feel that way.

You also can ask your family to help you develop self-advocacy skills that would transfer to other situations, such as getting together with friends at your home. Your family can help you prepare for spending time with your friends by running through different scenarios where self-advocacy skills can help you out. For example, say a friend from school comes over on a weekend. Once there, he says he wants to play one-on-one basketball. You don't feel comfortable playing basketball so you suggest another activity. He becomes angry and you don't know what to do next. Practicing these types of scenarios at home before your friend comes over allows you to be ready for this situation. You then can explain to your friend why you don't like to play basketball and why you suggested another activity. Hopefully, he will understand and you can then agree on a different activity.

REMEMBER THE POWER SELF-ADVOCACY

Now that you are aware of the concept of self-advocacy, you will quickly discover opportunities to use these strategies throughout the day. Using self-advocacy is almost like finding a power boost in your favorite video game adventure. You know that if you find one, you get a sudden boost to help you overcome obstacles and maybe even skip a level. By using the power of self-advocacy, you have a strategy that will help you overcome obstacles in everyday situations, and maybe even allow you to bypass the frustration and arguing that is usually part of the process and jump to a higher level—a workable solution.

Wrap Up: Tips and Tricks for Practicing Self-Advocacy

➤ **Self-advocacy means making those around you aware of your needs so that they will understand and support you.** Self-advocacy includes both asking for help, and explaining why you need to do certain things, and why it's OK. These things you need to do can include behaviors that are typical for people on the autism spectrum but might seem unusual to others, such as not maintaining eye contact or engaging in stimming behaviors.

➤ **To begin practicing self-advocacy in school, first find out if you have an IEP or 504 Plan, or other special plan.** If you do not, you can begin advocating for yourself by asking your parents to explore whether you might be eligible. If you do, make sure that you are an active participant in the decisions made about your education.

   ☛ Know what is on your IEP or 504 Plan, or other special plan.

   ☛ If you are in middle school or elementary school, you can partici-pate in your annual review meeting by sitting in for part of the time toward the end, and talking to the team about your needs and what strategies you think would help you.

   ☛ If you are in high school, you should attend the entire meeting. This is good practice for the self-advocacy that will be required of you as an adult.

➤ **Even without an IEP or 504 Plan, or other special plan, you can talk to your teachers when you need them to understand your point of view.** Remember that your teacher may not be able to speak with you immediately.

   ☛ Schedule a time to talk, during lunch or before or after class, when your teacher can give you his or her full attention.

   ☛ If you don't know what to say, you can practice with another adult.

   ☛ Be specific about your problems. Telling your teacher, "Math is hard," is not as helpful as explaining, "I'm having trouble lining up the numbers when I do long division and that's getting me confused."

   ☛ Make a list to help you remember the issues you want to discuss. You also can make a list of helpful strategies that you and your teacher come up with.

➤ **Self-advocacy can help combat bullying. Learn the difference between friendly teasing and bullying. Ask yourself these questions:**

   ☞ Is this person usually nice to you, or does he only tease you?

   ☞ Does he talk to everyone this way, or does he seem to be singling you out?

   ☞ Do you ever tease back? How does this person react if you do?

   ☞ If you tell this person that he hurt your feelings, does he apologize? Or does he continue to make fun of you?

   ☞ If an adult or another friend accuses this person of acting mean toward you, does he then try to blame you for his actions?

➤ **Use proactive and reactive self-advocacy strategies to help combat bullying.**

   ☞ Be aware of whether or not an area is supervised by adults.

   ☞ Look for options during recess.

   ☞ Work out a strategy with the adult in charge.

   ☞ Address the bully in a calm and direct manner.

   ☞ Try out a "comeback" line.

   ☞ Tell an adult.

➤ **Practice self-advocacy at home.** You can use self-advocacy to explain your point of view to your family and discuss compromises instead of getting into shouting matches. Your home also is a safe, comfortable environment for your family to help you practice advocacy skills to use in other situations.

CHAPTER 4

HOW CAN TECHNOLOGY HELP ME?

MISSION:
To identify programs and devices to meet your needs and your style.

As you learned in the last chapter, an important part of self-advocacy, whether at home or at school, involves calmly and respectfully stating your point of view. What happens when your point of view is based on perceptions that aren't really accurate? How can you help yourself when you find that you are continually misjudging something? You are about to learn how assistive technology (AT) can be your best friend.

Do these scenarios sound anything like your home?

Sam: "Mom, what time is karate?"

Mom: "You have been taking karate for a year, don't you know by now?"

Sam: "I've only been on the computer for 20 minutes."

Dad: "You've been on the computer for an hour. Please stop so we can eat dinner."

Sam: "This essay is too hard. I don't know where to start."

Mom: "Just sit down and think about what point you are trying to get across."

These are common dialogues for students with AS or NLD. Your family may get frustrated with your questions or misperceptions. You get frustrated with your family. It does not create happy relationships.

Assistive technology (AT) consists of tools that allow you to make things easier to do. Some AT tools are designed specifically for people with disabilities. Others serve to keep you organized. AT tools cover a variety of areas of difficulty for those who have AS or NLD. Those include:

➤ organization;
➤ time management;
➤ written language;
➤ reading comprehension, prediction, and summarizing; and
➤ math problem solving.

When a group of high school students with AS or NLD were asked whether they used a computer for school work or homework, they all responded yes. Surprisingly, when asked whether there were any software programs or websites they found helpful, their responses were very limited:

Alex, age 14: "Online dictionaries, Wikipedia"

Travis, age 16: "Wikipedia, dictionary. com"

Bill, age 15: "Wikipedia, dictionary. com"

Sean, age 17: "Wikipedia"

Mark, age 15: "Wikipedia to research"

> **What software programs or websites do you find helpful?**

> "Wikipedia, dictionary.com"

There is a whole world of hardware, software, and websites beyond dictionary.com and Wikipedia. You are about to learn that assistive technology can be a source of support, just like asking your parents the same question over and over, without any frustration. This chapter will give you some suggestions for helpful devices and programs. More information on all of the products listed here can be found in the Resources section in the back of this book.

Before running out and spending hundreds of dollars on fancy electronics, you must first identify your needs, which can be difficult. The needs you identify might really stem from a much larger picture. For instance, take Sam from the example at the start of this chapter. He has difficulty remembering what time his karate class, a recurring event, begins. Sam might think he should keep a calendar with the time of regular events. Even with that, he still doesn't remember. Let's use a flow chart to analyze Sam's issue (see Figure 2).

Once Sam realized that he was not remembering to look at his calendar, even an electronic one, he learned that he needed an audible timer. Now Sam does not have to depend on others to help him remember when an activity occurs.

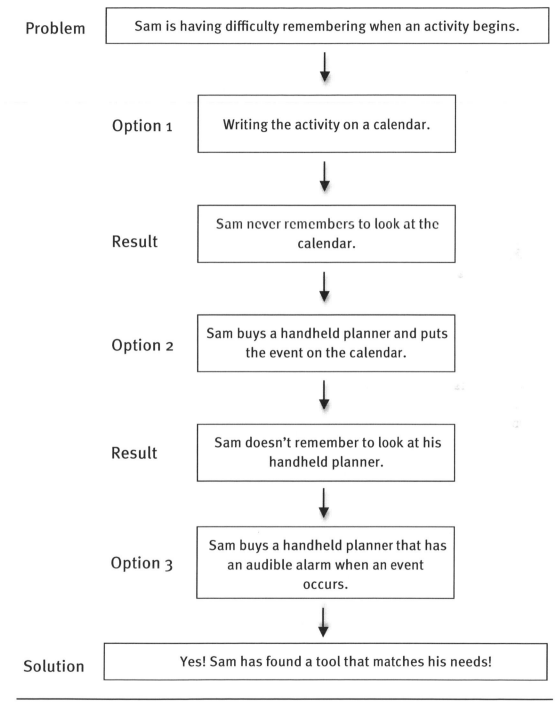

Figure 2. Finding the right technology flow chart.

TECHNOLOGY FOR ORGANIZATION AND FORGETFULNESS: THE PDA (PERSONAL DIGITAL ASSISTANT)

Of course, this is a student's dream. Who wouldn't want a cool handheld device? Devices that remind a person of an activity or task by making a noise are extremely popular. The benefits of using an electronic handheld device such as a Palm device or iPod touch include:

➤ calendars with audible sounds,
➤ address books,
➤ voice recorders,
➤ timers,
➤ appointment trackers,
➤ Internet access, and
➤ other downloadable applications.

There are some significant benefits to this type of AT. Some can sync between the device and a computer so that you only have to add the information in one place, but can access it in two. Some handheld devices offer additional downloads of other applications.

There also are some downsides. To begin with, they can be expensive. Secondly, because memory can be an issue for those with AS and NLD, remembering where you have put your device is really important. Some companies offer insurance on their devices, which you may want to consider. The last downside has to do with your personal habits. Ask yourself these questions:

➤ Are you disciplined enough to check the device on your own, at least daily?
➤ Will you remember to input the necessary information into the device?
➤ Will you be able to use the device effectively and not solely for games?

If the answer to all of these questions is yes, then here are some PDAs that you can consider:

➤ iPod touch and iPhone from Apple (see http://www.apple.com/store)
➤ Palm TX, Palm Z22, and Palm One Zire from Palm (see http://www.store.palm.com)

TECHNOLOGY FOR TIME MANAGEMENT: VISUAL AND AUDIBLE TIMERS

Now that Sam has found effective tools to help him remember when he is supposed to do things, he needs help learning to judge how long he has been working. Sam's mother complained that he was spending too much time on the computer, but Sam disagreed. This caused a lot of tension and arguing in the house. How could Sam prove to his parents that he was only on the computer for 20 minutes?

Many students with AS or NLD have difficulty with the concept of elapsed time. That includes judging how much time a task will take, and how much time they are spending on a task. Luckily, there are technologies that address both needs, and in the process make you aware of time management skills.

There are several electronic timers that allow you to track the length of time you are spending on a task. Once you identify patterns of how long tasks actually take, such as math homework, you can begin to create a realistic schedule for a day, week, or even a month.

Another type of timer visually represents the amount of time you have remaining to finish a task. One basic inexpensive technology is a simple kitchen or egg timer. Some make an audible click as each minute passes, so if you are easily distracted by noise, think carefully about this product. Others show a fading red circle; as time elapses the circle becomes smaller.

Digital timers with audible alerts include:
➤ Electronic handheld devices such as Palm or Apple products (see above)
➤ The WatchMinder (see http://www.watchminder.com)

➤ Timex Tween Digital (see http://www.timex.com/
Timex-Tween-Digital/dp/B000MAXWJY)

Visual timers that track the amount of time you are spending
on a task or the amount of time remaining on a task include:
➤ Online Stopwatch (see http://www.online-stopwatch.com)
➤ Time Timer (see http://www.timetimer.com)
➤ Time Tracker® Visual Timer & Clock (see http://www.
learningresources.com)
➤ TimeTracker v2.0 (see http://www.formassembly.com/
time-tracker)

TECHNOLOGY TO HELP WITH THE WRITING PROCESS: COMPUTERS AND WORD PROCESSORS

The process of writing incorporates many difficult skills for
those with AS or NLD. Writing requires many steps that include
organizing your thoughts, putting them down on paper, editing,
sequencing, and legibility. Because writing can be laborious for
those with AS or NLD, technology is essential. How many spelling
mistakes would you make if you did not have spellchecker? How
many times would you write a run-on sentence? If this sounds
familiar, you have many technological options.

Technology with built-in word processing program features
can be extremely valuable to students with AS or NLD. They allow
the freedom of making mistakes while writing and knowing you
can edit later, which can help with the flow of writing and assist
in written output. Your stress level will decrease when you take
syntax and other common writing errors out of the picture. This
is a safety net. If you are thinking of purchasing a computer for
this reason, make sure you look at all of the options, including
a laptop.

The better you are at keyboarding, the more useful a word
processor will be. If you are not a very good typist, there are a
number of programs that can help you develop this skill.

If a computer or word processor is not available, other options exist. A separate spellchecker device is less expensive and more portable. It can sit on your desk at school and fit in your backpack to take home. Because remembering to bring your spellchecker device home may be an issue, you may want to have one at home and one at school. Some students who have a computer at home use the spellchecker device at school.

Other devices, like the NEO or DANA, have the benefits of a word processing program but are less expensive and more portable. They are compatible with many Palm OS education applications as well. They can be set up to store each subject area in a separate location. All of the information that you input can be downloaded to a computer when attached with a cable. A downside to these devices is that they only let you see a limited number of lines at a time.

A tablet PC is another portable device that you can use to translate handwriting into a text document via a stylus that activates a touch screen. This is helpful if you are not fluent in keyboarding skills, as the program will learn your handwriting and translate it into text.

Some helpful portable word processors include:
➤ NEO and DANA (see http://www.neo-direct.com)
➤ QuickPAD IR (see http://www.quickpad.com)
➤ HP Touchsmart Tablet (see http://www.shopping. hp.com/series/category/notebooks/tx2z_series/3/ computer_store?jumpid=reg_R1002_USEN)

Some helpful word processing and spelling resources include:
➤ Microsoft Office (see http://www.office.microsoft.com)
➤ Children's Oxford Dictionary & Spell Checker (see http:// www.franklin.com/estore/dictionary/LWB-1216/)
➤ Spelling Ace® & Thesaurus (see http://www.franklin.com /estore/dictionary/SA-206S/)

Some popular keyboarding/typing programs include:
➤ Type to Learn (see http://www.sunburst.com)
➤ Typing Adventure (see http://www.typingadventure.com)
➤ GS Typing Tutor (see http://www.typingstar.com)

ORGANIZATIONAL SOFTWARE, SPEECH-TO-TEXT PROGRAMS, AND EVEN MORE WRITING

Don't you wish that there was a magic wand you could wave to instantly take your thoughts and transfer them into a coherent written product, such as an essay or letter? Our friend Sam does. He often doesn't know how to begin. Many students with AS or NLD tend to avoid tasks that involve writing, even simple tasks such as a thank-you note.

Why? First, who would want to do something that is so tremendously difficult for them? Second, writing is complicated for those with organizational issues. The process can be long because it involves brainstorming, prewriting, or drafting, using the draft to produce a cohesive written product, and then editing. You may then ask yourself, is it worth it? The use of technology is your magic wand that can ease this difficult process.

Word processing programs offer a variety of methods to organize your writing. They create outlines, including numerals and bullets, so you can get your thoughts down and then manipulate them as needed. These programs allow you the freedom to cut and paste your sentences or paragraphs if you need to change the order of events, or sequence your essay differently. You have the flexibility of changing your mind while you write.

Writing tablets are another kind of tool to allow you to get your thoughts down quickly and take notes in class. Writing tablets have all of the capabilities of a personal computer, but use handwriting-recognition software and a stylus to transform your illegible handwriting into a typed product. The downside is that they can be costly.

If you have difficulty finding the correct word to use (this is called **dysnomia**), a word prediction software program is the way to go. This type of program works

dysnomia: difficulty finding or remembering the correct word to use

with word processors and also predicts the word a person wants to enter into the computer. A person types the first letter of a word they are looking for and the program comes up with a list of possible words that begin with that letter. If you know the first few letters of the word you are writing, it can predict more complicated words by using yours as the root. Word prediction software also includes assistance with spelling, grammar, and syntax. One downside: These products may affect phonetic spellers. For example, if a person is trying to type the word "goal" and types in "gole," the program might not recognize the word.

Mind-mapping software is an amazing tool to help students organize their thoughts and then have the computer generate a written product based on their ideas. Many students with AS or NLD have difficulty getting their original ideas down on paper. Programs such as these allow students to express themselves, either orally or by typing into the computer. Thoughts from brainstorming transfer to an outline format to work from.

Speech-to-text programs offer students who have difficulty putting their thoughts down on paper an alternative. These programs allow you to speak into a microphone and see your words or sentences on the computer screen. This eliminates the handwriting component of writing. Once your thoughts are in the computer via a word processing program, they can be edited as necessary.

Some helpful writing software programs include:

➤ Co:Writer 6 word prediction software (see http://www.donjohnston.com/products/cowriter/index.html)
➤ Written Language Organizational Software
  ☞ Inspiration and Inspire Data (see http://www.inspiration.com)
  ☞ Draft:Builder 6 (see http://www.donjohnston.com/products/draft_builder/index.html)

➤ Speech-to-Text and Text-to-Speech Programs
  ☞ Kurzweil 3000 (see http://www.kurzweiledu.com)
  ☞ Write:OutLoud 6 (see http://www.donjohnston.com/products/write_outloud/index.html)
  ☞ WordQ and SpeakQ (see http://www.wordq.com)
  ☞ Dragon Naturally Speaking 10 (see http://www.m.nuance.com/dragon-solutions)
  ☞ MacSpeech (see http://www.macspeech.com)

TECHNOLOGY FOR NOTE TAKING

Because many students with AS or NLD have difficulty multitasking, taking notes from the board while listening to your teacher lecture proves difficult, if not impossible. Luckily there are options to reduce the stress that can be involved with note taking. As discussed in the above sections, word processor or writing tablet options are available. Schools are now becoming equipped with devices that can scan what is written on the white board into a computer and generate a hard copy. This is not a piece of technology that you can run out and buy for yourself, but making you aware of these options and having you share this with your parents or teachers may make a big difference.

Another option is to ask your teacher if you can tape-record in class. A small digital recorder can capture the lecture for you to study from later.

TECHNOLOGY FOR READING COMPREHENSION

Maggie, age 15, dreaded reading at school. Not the actual "reading," but having to demonstrate her understanding of the material. She had to read book after book of topics that did not interest her at all, and the pages were not easy to follow. Not only did she find the subjects boring, she had difficulty understanding what she was reading. There are many technologies out there to help students with AS or NLD to improve their reading comprehension.

Screen readers or electronic texts allow books, worksheets, or any other printed materials to be shown on a screen and usually are interactive. The advantages are limitless. Let's say you are reading a novel for language arts class. The book has been downloaded using a specialized software program, such as Kurzweil. The text will appear on the computer screen and you will be able to highlight the main ideas with one color while using a different color to highlight the supporting details.

You can choose how fast you would like the book or passage to be read to you or slow it down at specific places. Because issues with visual-spatial processing may make a cluttered screen confusing, you have the option of making the print larger in order to increase the amount of "white space" on the page. This type of software also can remember where you left off if you take a break from reading. Another plus: You can search for key words or characters and it will find the location in the book for you instead of flipping around in the book for what you are looking for. You can even click on a word you don't understand and hear the definition. Portable electronic texts such as e-books are very user friendly but can be very expensive. Other software programs are less expensive and can be installed at home or at school.

Some useful wireless reading devices and e-book programs include:

➤ Kindle (see http://www.amazon.com/Kindle)
➤ Sony Reader Digital Books (see http://www.sonystyle. com)
➤ eBooks.com (see http://www.ebooks.com)
➤ Nook (see http://www.barnesandnoble.com/ nook/?cds2Pid=30919)

TECHNOLOGY TO TACKLE MATH: SPEAKING CALCULATORS, INTERACTIVE ONLINE GAMES, AND SOFTWARE

Ugh! Another quiz today on math facts! It is very common for students with NLD, and even for some with AS, to have difficulty remembering their math facts, solving multistep problems, or understanding geometry concepts. Practicing with flashcards, quizzing yourself, and worksheets are not always effective and can even be boring. You may find that even after using all of these strategies, you are still failing your tests. Memorizing math facts is the foundation to move to more difficult units such as algebra, statistics, and calculus. How can you demonstrate your understanding of the broader concepts if you can't memorize your math facts? What kinds of tricks can you use to seal those facts into your memory? Have no fear, math technology is here! Software, online games, and tangible items await your arrival.

Many software and online companies offer free 30-day trials of their product, which gives you a chance to see how effective the product is. The fabulous feature of these programs and games is that they can target a specific skill and track progress. They also are geared toward different age groups, so you can eliminate more "cartoony" programs, if they don't appeal to you.

Other technologies are available that reinforce the skill of using a calculator. Talking calculators, for example, say the number as it is pressed into the calculator. They also read answers from the more difficult calculation problems. Hearing the numbers will help you recognize whether you have inputted the correct number.

Some helpful math resources include:
- Online Interactive websites (see http://www.mathbits. com and http://www.coolmath.com)
- Hardware
  - Talking Calculators (for some examples, see http:// www.maxiaids.com)
  - Math Pad and Math Pad Plus (see http://www. intellitools.com)

WHICH TOOL FOR WHICH SKILL?

Now comes the difficult part, matching your need to the right technology. Figure 3 is an example of matching up skills to the appropriate types of technology.

No matter what your need, assistive technology devices and programs can provide that extra bit of support to turn frustration into active creation!

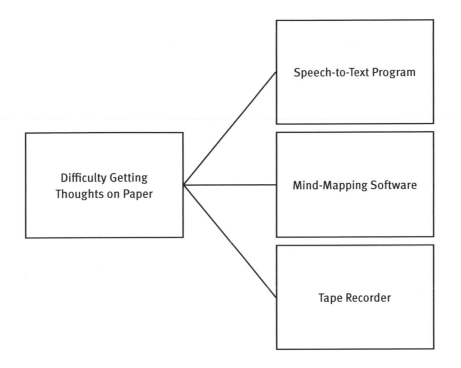

Figure 3. Sample organizer for choosing assistive technology.

Wrap Up: Tips and Tricks for Assistive Technology

➤ **Assistive technology consists of tools to make your life easier**. These can be devices or programs, and can help people with disabilities as well as those who just need more organization.

➤ **Before spending lots of money, make sure you identify your need.** An electronic calendar isn't really useful if you don't remember to look at it or program in events. Make sure you analyze what you really need to be successful before investing in AT.

➤ **For organization and forgetfulness, consider a handheld device.** There are some significant benefits to this type of AT. Some can sync between the device and a computer so that you only have to add the information in one place, but can access it in two. Some handheld devices offer additional downloads of other applications. The downside is that they can be expensive, and you must have the discipline to use them effectively.

➤ **Visual and audible timers can help with time management.** Timers can help you track how much time has passed, or determine how much is left to go. Audible timers give you reminders that you can hear, while visual timers show you elapsed or remaining time in a format you can see.

➤ **Computers and word processors help with the writing process.** Computers and word processing devices allow you to write freely, knowing that you can edit or spell-check later. They also remove the burden of handwriting from the writing process.

➤ **Organizational software and speech-to-text programs also can assist with writing.** Software programs are available to assist in almost all stages of the writing process, from turning your brainstorming sessions into cohesive outlines, to allowing you to dictate your ideas.

➤ **Use technology to take your notes.** Word processors and writing tablets can make note-taking easier. So can a small digital tape recorder. New technology available for classrooms may mean that your teacher can hand you a printout of notes on the white board.

➤ **Improve reading comprehension with electronic devices and software programs.** Although you may love to read, sometimes it can be hard to find the main idea or supporting details in school-assigned texts that don't interest you. Software programs that allow you to highlight as you go along, reduce the amount of text on the screen so you can concentrate better, or search for key terms electronically can help. So can portable electronic reading devices.

➤ **Math skills can be improved with assistive technology.** Software, online games, and even hardware such as talking calculators can improve math facts and lead to a deeper understanding of math concepts.

➤ **Match the right tool to the appropriate skill.** Use the flow chart in Figure 3 to help you match the right kind of assistive technology with the skill you need to improve.

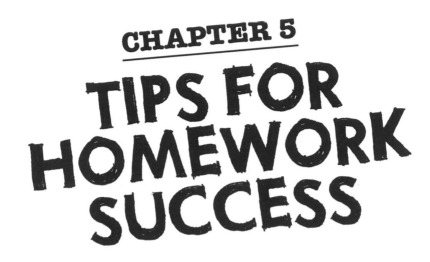

CHAPTER 5

TIPS FOR HOMEWORK SUCCESS

MISSION:
To develop an organizational system and strategies for managing homework.

L et's face it, nobody enjoys doing homework. If you had a choice of homework or playing on the computer, which would you choose? Unfortunately, homework is inevitable and there is no escape. Homework reinforces the lessons you learned at school. Teachers do not assign homework because they are mean. They want to give you opportunities to practice your newly learned skills. It also shows them what you know about the subject and gives you a chance to show off your knowledge. This chapter will teach you techniques to make your homework easier to tackle, and therefore more appealing. You never know, maybe one day you will choose doing your homework over playing on the computer.

BEFORE YOU BEGIN: FIND A WORKSPACE

In three easy steps, you can create a system to prioritize and keep track of your homework assignments. Before you do that, you should think about where you want to do your homework. Choose one place in the house, like your bedroom or the family room, as your designated homework space. It doesn't matter which room, but it should be free from distractions and there should be a desk or table where you can work. Equip your homework space with all of the supplies you will need for your assignments. This means paper, pencils and pens, markers and crayons, scissors and glue sticks, a stapler, ruler, and any other items or tools you regularly use. Having everything already in one spot will eliminate the time and stress of running through the house looking for materials during homework time. You can even purchase a special tray or supply box where you can keep everything together. Keep a homework folder that you can bring home and back to school. Place your finished homework inside as soon as it is done, so that you don't lose it or forget to take it with you to school. Now you are ready to learn to take charge of your assignments!

STEP 1: IDENTIFY YOUR STRENGTHS AND WEAKNESSES

Believe it or not, this important first step will give you the most insight into how to improve your homework skills. We all have tasks that are easier to do than others. One student with AS or NLD may have difficulty remembering to turn in her homework, even when it is done. Another student with AS or NLD might not know where to begin his homework when he gets home from school, while a third student with AS or NLD might be very set by routine and always have a specific time slot during the day allocated to homework.

As an example, a group of students ages 14–17 with AS and NLD were interviewed and shared some of the strategies they regularly used to help them be successful with homework. Their suggestions included many strategies that might seem contradictory, but they show that it's important to find a routine that works for you.

Travis, age 16: "Don't delay doing your homework."

Alex, age 14: "I have a soft drink and a snack before I start my homework."

Steve, age 16: "Go to after school homework club."

Alex, age 14: "Do your homework in a resource class or study hall."

Sean, age 17: "Do something little by little."

Travis, age 16: "Stick with it until you're finished."

What strategy do you use to help you be successful with homework?

"Don't delay doing your homework."

"I have a soft drink and a snack before I start my homework."

Which of these strategies work? The answer is, all of them. You need to find the one that is right for you and matches your strengths with your challenges.

It can be frustrating in the beginning, but you will be more successful with your homework by developing a positive attitude.

This may not happen overnight, but it can happen as you learn ways to compensate for tasks that are difficult for you. Feeling positive about yourself and recognizing your strengths as well as your needs will go a long way toward changing your attitude about homework.

Take a few minutes to identify your strengths and needs using the chart in Figure 4. If you can't think of any strengths or needs off the top of your head, think about what you like to do and what you hate doing. Most people like to do things that come easily, and don't like to do things that are difficult for them.

Things That Come Easy to Me	Things That Are Harder for Me

Figure 4. Understanding strengths and needs chart.

Once you have a list of tasks that are easy and tasks that are difficult, you can use that knowledge to prioritize your homework. Some people prefer to get the difficult assignment out of the way first, and know that they can coast for the rest of the time. Others like to start off with the easy assignments to build success and feel more confident. A third option is to alternate easy and difficult assignments to give you a built-in break. Identify which method works for you, and prioritize your homework accordingly.

STEP 2: MANAGE YOUR TIME

People with AS or NLD often have difficulty with elapsed time. For example, 10 minutes of homework might feel like an hour. Using the strategies in this chapter, you will learn how to determine how long a homework task will take, from how long it takes you to study for each subject to learning how to pace yourself with longer projects. You will learn what an hour feels like and what you can accomplish in that time. You will even learn how different tasks take more time than others.

Between afterschool activities and other obligations, it is difficult to find a consistent time for homework, especially if you do not like doing it in the first place. It becomes your last priority even though it should be your first. Although your school might give you a planner, it cannot tell you how long an assignment might take, the time you will need to study for a test, or how to manage a long-term assignment such as a research report.

HOW CAN YOU FIGURE OUT HOW MUCH TIME YOU ARE SPENDING ON AN ASSIGNMENT?

That's the easy part. To monitor how much time it takes to finish different tasks, such as studying for a subject (the amount of time may change based on the subject) or completing a worksheet, you can use some of the following time management strategies that were reviewed in the previous chapter:

➤ Use a simple kitchen timer, or set the timer on your microwave.
➤ Use an audible or visual timer device.
➤ Install a program that allows you to see how much time you have been working on the computer.

You also can try another fun strategy to help you with time management and elapsed time:

➤ Next time you have a homework assignment that looks like it will take forever, make a guess about how long you think it will take to complete. Write down your guess. Then, use a timer to track how long it actually takes to finish your assignment. Chances are, it will take less time than you predicted. Do this a few times, and you will begin to get a better sense of how much time you need to allow yourself for homework.

Record the amount of time you spend on each subject, per day, on a time-tracker chart, like the one in Figure 5.

STEP 3: CREATE A SCHEDULE THAT WORKS FOR YOU

Once you identify your needs and determine what assignments or activities you are expected to do and how long they will take, the next step is putting it all together. There are many methods of keeping a planner. Two are addressed below.

USING MONTHLY AND WEEKLY CALENDARS

A monthly calendar gives a more global perspective. It will help you identify patterns in your schedule, track due dates for long-term assignments, and help you determine how to pace yourself. This method can be very effective if it's kept simple and used properly.

A weekly calendar will make you aware of how much time you can allocate each day to do your homework. Because some obligations change weekly, it allows you to budget your time in a more channeled way.

Remember to take advantage of the assistive technology programs and devices listed in Chapter 4. You can use calendars on your computer or handheld device, send yourself reminder e-mails, or enter recurring events so you don't have to copy from one week to another.

No matter which method you choose, the hardest part may be to remember to input the information into the calendar.

This is a work in progress. You may need to try many different systems until you find what works for you. Use the steps below to help you create monthly and weekly calendars.

Week of _____

Subject	Monday	Tuesday	Wednesday	Thursday	Friday	Weekend

In each box, write down the assignment you completed and how long it took you to complete.

Figure 5. Homework time tracker.

Create a monthly calendar.

1. Choose one color pen, such as blue, to fill in your set activities such as clubs, religious school, or any other special plans you may have.
2. Choose a different color, such as purple, to represent any special days such as no school, holiday, and so on.
3. Finally, choose a third color, such as red, to write in your tests and quizzes and assignments.

Figure 6 shows you what a finished monthly calendar might look like. Remember, your calendar will be more colorful than ours!

Create a weekly calendar.

1. Start with the time you get home from school.
2. Choose one color and fill in your set activities such as clubs, religious school, or any other special plans you may have. If you have already created a monthly calendar, use the same colors.
3. Choose a different color for other commitments such as times for family dinners.
4. Outline in pen the empty blocks of time in 30 or 45 minute intervals. For middle school, you may want to estimate at least one hour per day for homework, while high school students may need at least 2 hours.
5. You also will need to fill in two blocks of 15 minutes each for planned breaks.
6. Remember to give yourself about 15 minutes to rest when you get home from school. Have a snack, and get your materials ready.

Let's look more closely at your empty blocks of time. The goal is to maximize those blocks to work on your homework, which

Sunday	Monday	Tuesday	Wednesday	Thursday	Friday	Saturday
	10/1	10/2	10/3	10/4	10/5	10/6
	English Paper Due		Math Test	Karate	Science Quiz	Movies With Jack
	Religious School		Math Tutor		Clubs	
10/7	10/8	10/9	10/10	10/11	10/12	10/13
	Religious School	English Quiz	History Paper Due	Karate	Science Quiz	Family Trip
			Math Tutor		Clubs	
10/14	10/15	10/16	10/17	10/18	10/19	10/20
Family Trip	No School	English Test	Math Tutor	History Report Due	Science Quiz	
	Family Trip			Karate	Math Test	
					Clubs	
10/21	10/22	10/23	10/24	10/25	10/26	10/27
	History Test		Math Quiz	Karate	No School	Movies With Jack
	Religious School		Math Tutor			
10/28	10/29	10/30	10/31	11/1	11/2	11/3
My Birthday!	Religious School	Math Test	Research Project Due	Karate	Science Quiz	
			Halloween		Math Test	
					Clubs	

Figure 6. Sample monthly calendar.

will include studying for tests or quizzes. Some students need to work subject by subject and some work in smaller increments of time, while others like to get it out of the way. Students with AS or NLD tend to need breaks. Figure 7 shows you what a weekly calendar might look like with everything blocked out, including time for breaks.

	Monday	Tuesday	Wednesday	Thursday	Friday
3:30 – 3:45	Break	Break	Math Tutor	Break	Clubs
3:45 – 4:30	HW	HW	Math Tutor	HW	HW
4:30 – 4:45	Break	Break	Break	Break	Break
4:45 – 5:30	Religious School	HW	HW	Finish HW	HW
5:30 – 6:30	Religious School	Free if finished with HW	15 minute break, then HW	15 minute break, then HW	Free if finished with HW
6:30 – 7:30	Dinner	Dinner	Dinner	Dinner	Dinner
7:30 -8:00	HW	Free if finished with HW	Free if finished with HW	Karate	Weekend!

Figure 7. Sample weekly calendar.

HELPFUL HINTS FOR MANAGING ASSIGNMENTS

1. When you have an assignment that is due in 3 days or more, put the name of the project on both the day that it is assigned and on the due date on your weekly calendar.
2. Now allot enough time per day to work on that assignment.
   a. In order to complete this step, you need to take the assignment and break it down into pieces.
   b. For example, say a project is due in 4 days that requires you to research a country and write a report based on what you have

learned. The first thing you would do (after writing it on your calendar) is to determine how many steps would be needed to finish this project. You may need one night for research, one night to begin writing, and the third night to finish writing and edit.

c. Write each step on your calendar.

HOMEWORK AND SELF-ADVOCACY

What happens when you do your homework, but forget to turn it in? How does that make you feel? Maybe the following scenario is familiar:

Now that I've finished my homework, put it in my binder, and brought it to school, it ends up in my backpack the entire day so I don't get credit for the assignment. I've worked so hard on this assignment and am too embarrassed to go to my teacher. She will just tell me that I am old enough to remember to turn it in myself. My parents told me that I should advocate for myself or speak up for myself. I should remind the teacher that I need prompting. I know I need to speak up for myself, but it is too hard.

You've put all of that work into your assignment, and now you need to make sure it is turned in. In Chapter 3, you learned about ways to approach your teacher and advocate for yourself. Here are some additional self-advocacy strategies to make sure your homework gets handed in:

➤ Use a homework folder, and put your homework in it as soon as it's finished.

➤ Ask your teacher to help you, either with verbal reminders or with a signal, to turn in your homework for at least 2 weeks until it becomes part of your routine, which it will.

➤ Have your teacher place a sticky note on your desk before class. Once you sit down, the note will remind you to turn in your assignment.

➤ In an ideal situation, there would be a reminder on the board for all students to see.

➤ Keep track of the assignments you are responsible for turning in. Some schools have programs that report your completed and missing assignments. Put that on your weekly calendar to make it part of your routine.

STARTING A WRITING TASK

Getting started on an assignment that involves writing can be difficult for students with AS or NLD. There are several strategies that will allow you to get your thoughts down in an organized manner. Take this scenario: You are given a writing prompt and are allowed to choose any format, such as an essay, play, or song, to answer the prompt. Even though you are allowed to choose the format, it still can be difficult to begin the assignment. Many teachers may think that because you are allowed to choose your product, you will not need any help organizing the information. More often than not, you will still need to organize your thoughts, which is why strategies are needed.

One strategy is to create a graphic organizer, such as a story map, to help organize your thoughts. Create one that works for you. Another strategy is to use assistive technology. As you discovered in Chapter 4, there also are computer programs that allow you to type in key words and the program puts them into outline or paragraph formats, such as Inspiration (http://www.inspiration.com), which uses both pictures and words to create a web. Icons allow the web to turn into either an outline or essay. Another method would be to go right to the computer to get all your thoughts out. Then you can cut and paste your ideas into the correct sequence. You have to find out which method works for you. Remember, there is no "one size fits all" format to organize one's thoughts.

PUTTING IT ALL TOGETHER

By using all of the above strategies, over time you will learn to identify your strengths and weaknesses, estimate the amount of time your homework will take, create a schedule, and manage assignments. You will even be armed with self-advocacy strategies to remember to turn in completed assignments. Suddenly, homework doesn't seem so overwhelming, does it? It's easier to develop a positive attitude when you have taken that first step to gain control over your homework issues. Maybe tonight you will choose to do that assignment before playing on the computer!

Wrap Up: Tips and Tricks for Managing Homework

➤ **Create an organized workspace.** Choose one place in your home as your designated homework space. Make sure you have all of the supplies you will need for your assignments.

➤ **Identify your strengths and weaknesses, and use that knowledge to prioritize your assignments.** Things that you are good at will probably take less time to do than things you find challenging. Decide whether you want to do your most challenging work first, last, or alternate it with easier assignments.

➤ **Manage your time.** Use timers, assistive technology programs and devices, and other strategies to help monitor how much time it takes to do different tasks. You will begin to get a realistic sense of how long certain homework assignments take.

➤ **Create a schedule that works for you.** Create weekly charts to keep track of your day-to-day assignments and activities. Monthly charts give you the big picture so that you know what's coming up. You can use a chart system, or you can input the information into a computer or handheld device.

➤ **Use self-advocacy strategies to remember to turn in completed assignments.** Explain your need for reminders to the teacher and work out a system in class, such as verbal or visual reminders, to turn in homework.

➤ **Use a variety of strategies to begin a writing assignment.** When you don't know how to begin to answer a writing prompt, turn to organizational strategies for a variety of methods to get your thoughts out. Simple graphic organizers or assistive technology programs can help you outline your ideas.

➤ **Take control and develop a positive attitude.** Using the above steps helps you take control over your homework so that assignments won't seem so overwhelming. As things become easier and more manageable, you also might start to feel better about the whole process.

CHAPTER 6

TIPS FOR CLASSROOM SUCCESS

MISSION:

To identify your needs in the classroom and create a plan of attack to meet those needs.

LEFT-HANDED SCISSORS

Having AS or NLD means that you are going to need to approach some classroom-related tasks differently than neurotypical students. It also may mean that your teacher needs to make some allowances for your learning style. This isn't a big deal. To some degree, everyone needs to find ways to compensate for individual differences. Every year, more and more is written about AS and NLD. As more people are made aware of these disabilities and are sensitized to the needs of students with AS and NLD, it will become easier to advocate for yourself and put strategies for classroom success into practice.

Consider people who are left-handed. Back when your grandparents went to school, it was very challenging to be a lefty. Doing things left-handed was considered wrong and students actually were forced to use their right hands to write, even if it was very difficult for them. Things changed in the next generation. When your parents went to school, everyone realized that it was all right to be a lefty. That's just how some people were born. Tools like left-handed scissors became standard in classrooms, and left-handed baseball gloves (which are worn on the right hand) were stocked in P.E. class. Today's classroom is even more progressive. In place of left-handed scissors, many classrooms now stock ambidextrous scissors that can be used with either hand. Perhaps as time moves on, educators also will be more aware of the needs of those with autism and related disorders. Things that you need to advocate for today may become standard practice in the classroom of the future, making learning more accessible for all types of students.

Until then, here are some strategies that you can use to help with challenges in the classroom environment.

STRATEGY: YOUR PLAN OF ATTACK

The term *strategy* is very generic; it covers a wide range of skills. In reality, a strategy is a plan of attack. It is an organized way to achieve a goal. Before you go to bed at night, you should try to determine if there will be a situation the next day that will require a specific strategy or plan of attack. The key word is "if." How are you supposed to know when you will need to use a strategy, and how do you know which one to use? Strategies need to be based on skills or strengths. For example, if technology is your strength and you are supposed to write a lengthy essay in history class, you may choose to ask the teacher if you could do a PowerPoint presentation instead. You actually are using two strategies, technology and self-advocacy. Effective strategies also include an element of self-awareness. For example, if you notice that it is more difficult for you to do homework with music on than without, you are being self-aware. Next time you will know not to put music on. Why is this important? Knowing how you learn and knowing what strategies work the best for you can only increase your successes.

HOW TO RECOGNIZE WHEN A STRATEGY IS NEEDED

In the last chapter, you were able to figure out your strengths and weaknesses in homework by making a list of what you liked and what you didn't like. You learned that most of the time, people don't like things that are difficult for them. The same rule applies to class work. The most difficult parts of your school day, the parts you don't like, are the first places you should look at to see if you could develop a better plan of attack.

These students with AS or NLD thought about what the most difficult part of their school day was, and why:

Chris, age 13: "The most difficult part of my school day is getting there because it's the early morning and you have to readjust to being there."

Brian, age 10: "The most difficult part of my school day is math class because I have to take quizzes, tests and a lot of other stuff, and I have to do multiplication.

What is the most difficult part of your day and why?

"Taking tests. I study for what seems like hours, but sometimes I don't fully understand the question being asked."

Amy, age 15: "Taking tests. I study for what seems like hours, but sometimes I don't fully understand the question being asked."

It is not uncommon to fail many times, or to feel like you don't want to have anything to do with a subject before realizing other ways to work through a situation. For example, you study from your notes at home before a social studies test but still fail. You do not understand why; you studied and studied. Then one day, you look over and notice your neighbor's notes looking very different from yours. You are not comfortable asking to see her notes so you decide to watch what she does during class. You notice that she is copying from the board and taking notes at the same time. Hey, that's too hard! So what can you do?

Let's look at your options. First, you could do nothing and keep studying from your notes and failing tests. Second, you could ask your neighbor for a copy of her notes (a possibility, yet a little scary), or lastly, you could figure out a way to get the same information as your neighbor. Now put together some of your strengths and advantages, such as sitting in front of the class and using the computer. There is no way you think you will be able to write all that information down in that short period of time, as you're too busy listening to the teacher. What could possibly allow you to listen to the lecture later so you can pay attention to what the teacher is saying now? How about getting permission from your teacher to tape-record the class? YES! That is it! You will receive the teacher's notes (as before) and tape-record the lecture. When you get home, you will listen to the class and then add to your notes. There is no rush. Figure 8 illustrates this formula—develop your strategy by thinking about your areas of strength.

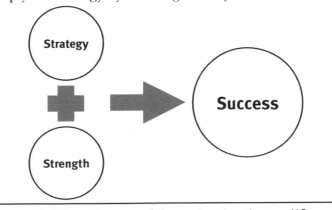

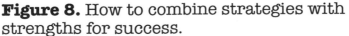

Figure 8. How to combine strategies with strengths for success.

IDENTIFYING YOUR NEEDS
IN THE CLASSROOM

The hardest part of using a strategy is finding the right one to use and knowing when to use it. School areas that may be more difficult for those with AS and NLD could include:

1. Learning how to work with classroom systems
2. Organizing materials
3. Group activities
4. Taking notes
5. Taking tests
6. Math
7. Reading comprehension
8. Writing
9. Keeping up with the pace of the class
10. Multitasking
11. Staying relaxed at school

AREA OF NEED 1: LEARNING HOW TO WORK WITH CLASSROOM SYSTEMS

In middle school and high school, you may encounter up to seven different teachers a day. That can be intimidating for anyone, let alone a student with AS or NLD. By far, this is the most important area for school success. How can you be expected to succeed if you are in an environment where you can't perform? Would a doctor perform surgery in a movie theater? No!

In the beginning of the school year it is important to find out key information about each teacher, such as where you will be expected to turn in your homework or the type of notes you will be required to take. This is sometimes referred to as the "hidden curriculum," or the unwritten rules and expectations of the class. Learning what these are can make understanding classroom procedures easier. Classroom systems or procedures can include:

➤ Seating arrangements
➤ How and where to turn in assignments
➤ What materials you are expected to bring to class (you should write this in your agenda or assignment book)

➤ The procedures for copying down homework into your agenda book

☛ Do you need to copy the assignments completely, or just use key words? You may find that key words won't be enough for you to remember the assignment.

☛ Make sure you have a back-up plan, like using the school's online assignment system.

➤ What to do if your assignment is late

➤ Knowing the curriculum and what is expected of you

☛ Requesting a syllabus if you don't already have one.

☛ Knowing the objective of the lesson. Is it being clearly written on the board, or do you need clarification from the teacher?

Finding out this information either before school begins (recommended) or on the first day of school will greatly reduce the number of missed assignments during the school year.

AREA OF NEED 2: ORGANIZING MATERIALS

The transition from elementary school to middle school is tremendous. The transition from middle school to high school is intense. You will need to develop a flexible strategy to organize your materials. You may have to use trial and error until you find the one that works with your learning style. A teacher might give you 10 suggestions of how to organize your binder, but none may fit your style. Although suggestions are welcome and helpful, you need to own your system.

Simple ways to stay organized include deciding which system works best for each person. Some suggestions include:

➤ Decide if it would be better to use one notebook per subject or use a binder with color-coded tabs and folders.

➤ If using a binder, consider using two instead, one for your morning classes and one for your afternoon classes.

➤ If using a binder, buy one folder per subject (color-coded) to put your loose papers in.

➤ Use a separate folder or binder section for homework, keeping it all in one place.

➤ Use a pencil case to hold loose supplies.

➤ Remember your assistive technology options, and use an electronic organizer for your assignments and due dates.

➤ Use the calendar system you learned in Chapter 5 to keep track of long-term assignment due dates.

➤ Each evening, create a to-do list for the next day. Review it in the morning and then again at lunch.

➤ Keep an extra set of books at home.

➤ Ask the teacher to confirm that you have the assignment written down correctly and in the correct location.

➤ In the front of your binder or notebook for each class, tape a list of your needed materials for that class that you can refer to.

AREA OF NEED 3: GROUP ACTIVITIES

You walk into biology class and hear the teacher say, "Today in biology, you will be working in groups of four to complete the lab assignment." Upon hearing this, you may panic at first, but you realize that you have no choice but to participate. Group work can be very difficult, because you need to rely on the skills of others and you might not know what to expect. The dynamics of communicating with a group, including the subtleties of non-verbal communication, can be very challenging. There are always going to be times where you will have to be in groups. Don't panic—create a plan of attack instead. Strategies can include:

➤ Let your teacher know that you need advance notice of when you will be working with others in order to reduce any anxiety.

➤ Ask your teacher if you could be paired with a specific student you know understands your strengths and needs.

➤ Ask the group to spend 5 minutes discussing who will be responsible for which parts of the assignment.

➤ Choose a role that would fit your strength, such as the organizer. Ask your group politely if you can volunteer to do that job.

AREA OF NEED 4: TAKING NOTES

Everyone would agree that taking notes would not be his or her first choice of activities, but it is probably one of the most important components for school success. Taking notes does not only mean a student sitting at her desk copying down every word the teacher says. It is more practical and streamlined. Students with AS or NLD know that writing can be laborious, so it is understandable how this process can seem overwhelming. Additionally, it can be difficult to interpret the meaning of everything that is being said, especially if a teacher uses lots of metaphors and figures of speech.

Strategies can help here, too. Some things you can try:

➤ Record the class and transcribe or review the lesson later.
➤ Get copies of the teacher's notes or lesson prior to the beginning of class.
➤ Get a copy of another student's notes.
➤ Ask the teacher for a note-taking graphic organizer that has key concepts filled in.
➤ If given a worksheet, underline or highlight the key terms being discussed.
➤ Use technology such as a portable keyboard or other devices or programs you learned about in Chapter 4.
➤ If the pace of the lecture is too quick, write down as many key words as you can. If it is too difficult to figure out what the key words are, then you should speak with your teacher about alternate methods.
➤ If you are a visual thinker, another way to keep up with the pace is to make visual representations of key concepts, using a symbol or icon, instead of writing down the words.

AREA OF NEED 5: TAKING TESTS

Have you ever thought to yourself: "There's no point in studying for my science exam. First, I won't know half the answers, and second, I won't have enough time to finish the test."

Don't be so hard on yourself. Test taking is a very difficult skill. (Yes, it is a skill.) Tests are not all the same; they come in a variety of formats, which require a variety of skills. The most common types of tests are essay, multiple-choice, matching, and fill in the blank. Clearly, the writing component will take the longest amount of time to complete, so estimating the amount of time each section will take when combined is difficult. Before a test, request a study guide from your teacher about the topic.

General strategies you can use include:

➤ Be on time for class.

➤ Read all of the directions first.

➤ Skip the more difficult questions and come back to them later.

➤ Wear a watch or make sure the room has a clock to help manage your time.

➤ Go back and review your answers.

➤ If you finish early (which you shouldn't), go back and check your answers again.

➤ Plan with the teacher ahead of time of what to do if you do not finish the test.

➤ Wear comfortable clothing.

Multiple-choice test strategies include:

➤ Cover up the choices immediately before reading the question. See if you can then answer the question without having the choices in front of you. This way, you are certain of your answer and will not second-guess yourself.

➤ If needed, put the question in your own words.

➤ If filling in a test with bubbles, make sure you double-check that the problem you are answering has the same number as the circle you are filling in. Better yet, see if you would be allowed to circle the answers right in the text booklet. You will need prior permission for this.

Essay test strategies include the following:

➤ Use a word processor.

➤ Estimate the amount of time you will need for this section and complete it last.

➤ Paraphrase in your mind what is expected of you from this question.

AREA OF NEED 6: MATH

Imagine a world where instead of math symbols like + or − there were colors to prompt you what to do or where every number you wrote matched exactly up with the number below it. No, it's not a dream and can actually happen with the right strategies and accommodations.

Take Duncan, age 12, who spent countless hours trying to memorize his facts. He tried flashcards, grids, and calculators but still could not quickly recall $5 \times 6 = 30$. He didn't want the other kids to see him counting on his fingers so he would just sit there and not do anything, especially when the teacher made the class take frustrating fact tests where you had to answer 50 math facts on one page within a minute. The next year, Duncan had a new math teacher who used music and rhymes to teach multiplication facts. Guess what? Duncan learned all of his facts within 2 months.

Math can be difficult on many levels for those with AS or NLD. Because fine-motor skills are difficult, writing numbers within a specific space that have to line up can be next to impossible. Discriminating between the different symbols for the operations, as well as operations that involve multiple steps such as long division or algebraic equations, creates another layer of challenge. Spatial difficulties also can affect telling time using an analog clock and learning geometry. Do you hate when a teacher asks you to estimate an answer? Esti-what? Don't they understand that you don't see a point in guessing when you will eventually have to figure out the answer? Hopefully by now you have realized that you can learn strategies to help you in all of these challenging areas. There are even strategies to help you weed out the important information from the unimportant information in word problems.

Do you learn better by hearing or seeing the information? If you are diagnosed with NLD, chances are you need to hear the logic. If you are diagnosed with AS, you might think more in pictures, visual diagrams, and representations. Don't think for one minute about letting these obstacles get in the way of learning math.

Strategies to improve your math skills include:
- ➤ Use graph paper to help line up numbers in an equation.
- ➤ Instead of copying the problem onto a separate sheet of paper, ask for a copy of that page from the text and staple

it to the graph paper with just a reference to the number instead of a copy of the entire problem.

➤ A calculator can be your best friend.

➤ Use a multiplication chart (or addition, subtraction, and division charts for that matter).

➤ Ask the teacher if you could show your work for a limited number of problems.

➤ Use a digital clock instead of an analog clock.

➤ Ask your teacher to explain how to do a problem using her words and not just having you read it from the text.

➤ Instead of flashcards, use a system that puts the facts to music, like Schoolhouse Rock.

➤ Assign a color to represent each operation. For example, ask your teacher (or you can do this) to highlight all of the addition symbols red, subtraction symbols blue, multiplication symbols yellow, and division symbols green. Then when you are working through algebraic equations, you won't add instead of multiplying.

➤ Multistep math tasks such as long division need to be broken down into steps.

➤ Word problems need to be presented in limited amounts. You should request if you could explain your answer orally instead of in writing.

➤ When given a word problem, underline key words such as "all together," "difference," or "sum," to help sort out what the problem is asking you to solve.

AREA OF NEED 7: READING COMPREHENSION

Randy, a 13-year-old with AS, loves to read anything he can get his hands on. He reads mostly science fiction and some fantasy. Although Randy is a strong reader with a good vocabulary, if you were to ask Randy how a character was feeling in the story, you may not get the answer you would expect. Randy would probably answer, "How should I know how he's feeling?" Randy might accurately describe the character's actions, but not realize why the character was acting that way. Why does this happen when Randy is such a good reader? Randy may be reading, but he is not making inferences from the text. He is not making predictions or drawing conclusions and understandably, this can be very frustrating. Just like writing, reading has three distinct purposes: reading for information (nonfiction), reading to perform a task (like a recipe), and reading for literary experience (fun). Knowing your purpose before reading is key.

Just like Randy, you may find understanding what you are reading at a deeper level difficult. One reason can be the author's use of language. For black and white thinkers and learners, abstract reasoning is more challenging. Let's take idioms as an example. While reading a science fiction book, you come across the phrase "A leopard can't change its spots" and you think to yourself, "I'm reading a book about the future, there are no leopards here!" What the author really means is that people don't change.

You will notice that this area of need does not include **decoding**, or the ability to put together sounds to make words. That usually comes easy for students with AS or NLD. Reading comprehension, making sense from written material, is what is difficult. Reading comprehension has a lot of subskills such as making inferences, determining the main idea, or recognizing subtle messages. There are many more skills a person needs in order to be successful in his understanding of written text.

decoding: translating a printed word into sounds by matching letters or a sequence of letters to their corresponding sounds

The two forms of comprehension are literal and inferential. Literal refers to the "right there" questions, such as who is the main character or where the story takes place. Inferential questions are more difficult for the student with AS or NLD. Cecile Cyrul Spector's book, *Between the Lines: Enhancing Inferencing Skills* (2006), discussed the importance of learning skills to improve your inferential comprehension. Figuring out when and where an event in a story takes place and making the connection between a character's action and its consequence are vital when reading.

One strategy, locating key words and phrases, can help improve your inferential comprehension. Key words provide clues to help figure out what is happening in the text that isn't directly stated. Sometimes this is called "reading between the lines." For example, suppose a character in a story says, "Even though we were all wearing sunglasses, I could feel their eyes staring at me." Given that sentence, what key words or phrases can you find to help you figure out that the story takes place during the day? If you answered "sunglasses," you are correct. Let's try one more. From the following sentence, see if you can figure out where this story is taking place: "Jenna took off her winter coat, placed her skis and boots on the rack, and drank a cup of hot chocolate in front of the fireplace." The key words would include winter coat, skis, and boots, which will help you realize that the story probably takes place somewhere cold and snowy in winter.

Beyond reading between the lines, if you have difficulties with visual-spatial processing, the actual lines of text themselves may sometimes be difficult to track. You may frequently lose your place in a book that has very small type, for example. There are tools available to help you compensate for this need. One is the use of a highlighter strip. These are colored translucent strips that get placed over a line or set of lines in text to help with tracking. You also could use an index card to help track where you are in the book.

In the written expression section, you learned about using graphic organizers to help with prewriting. A similar strategy can be applied to assist in reading comprehension. Now that we have discussed what reading comprehension is and why it is difficult, let's focus on ways to make it easier.

Before reading:

➤ Know why you are reading.
➤ If possible, choose books that have a lot of "white space" on the page to help with your visual-spatial needs. Sometimes the library may have books considered large print that have more white space.
➤ Know the genre of your text. This will help with your connection to the text.
➤ Read the back of the book first and then skim through the chapter titles if they are available.

➤ Try to find a study guide if possible. You can check the library, search online, or ask your teacher.

During reading:
➤ Use a visual highlighter or index card to help with your tracking.
➤ At the end of each chapter or unit, write at least two sentences about the events that happened. (You can use technology to help you!) Use this to help keep a sequential list of the events of the story.
➤ Keep a list of the main characters as they are introduced, and how they change during the story.
➤ Some students get "highlighter happy" and once they start highlighting they can't stop. Before they know it, the entire paragraph is in a different color. Instead, try underlining with a pencil. By placing the pencil under the word instead of highlighting on top of it, you are able to read what will be coming next. It also allows you to erase if needed.
➤ Keep a dictionary next to you and look up any unknown words that you can't figure out using context clues or words that would give you clues to the unknown word's meaning.
➤ Remember to look for key words and phrases that give you clues to what might be going on in the text that isn't directly stated.

After reading:
➤ Read it again.
➤ Review your notes.
➤ Talk to another person about what you have just read.
➤ Compare your understanding of the text to that of your peers.

Because students with AS or NLD have difficulty with summarizing and answering inferential questions, how can the teacher know that you understood the text? Multiple-choice quizzes would help you by providing the right answer as one of the choices. Fill-in-the-blank quizzes would help you by providing the context for finding the right answer. This would be a good time to review the section on test-taking and study skill strategies.

AREA OF NEED 8: WRITING

The process of writing can be overwhelming, from the act of handwriting to the organization, and finally, the end result of a written product. Why is writing so difficult for students with AS or NLD? Difficulties with planning, making inferences, and determining which ideas are more important than others can be obstacles in developing writing skills. Writing requires a lot of original thinking and connecting it to abstract concepts. Additionally, problems with visual-spatial processing affect not only handwriting, but also writing in general.

The truth is, writing can be made more manageable when broken down into easy-to-understand steps. For example, did you know that there are many types of writing? Writing to inform, persuade, and for personal experience are the three most common reasons we write. By recognizing the purpose of your writing, you have jumped the first hurdle. One mnemonic device that can be helpful when preparing to write is FAT-P:

Form—Are you writing a letter, essay, advertisement, or poem?
Audience—Who is your audience? If you are writing a letter, who do you expect to be reading it?
Topic—What is the main idea?
Purpose—Are you writing to inform, to persuade, or to express personal ideas?

Remember that the more structured your writing task is, the better.

Before your hands touch your pencil or keyboard, there are a couple of items you should definitely have. The first is a rubric or outline of what is expected of you for the writing project. The second is a self-editing checklist to use during the revising stage.

Handwriting is the most obvious obstacle for a student with AS or NLD when it comes to the act of writing. This can be addressed in a variety of ways:

➤ A handwriting method such as the Handwriting Without Tears™ program that can teach you strategies to make the physical process of writing easier.
➤ Use of a pencil grip.

➤ Special handwriting paper with a raised midline (it looks like regular paper).

➤ Use of graph paper to help line your numbers up correctly for math problems.

➤ Use of assistive technology, such as a word processor, spell-checker device, or even a tape recorder to dictate your responses and transcribe them later.

As writing demands increase, the technology possibilities are endless in regards to what is available to students. Remember to consider all of the options outlined in Chapter 4.

The first stage in the writing process is called prewriting. This is where all of the thoughts swirling around in your head are magically supposed to appear on your nice clean piece of paper. It probably doesn't happen quite like that, does it? If you are like most students with AS or NLD, you probably find it difficult to generate your own topics or to "free write." You probably prefer rules and structure. If so, typical graphic organizers such as webs are probably not the best strategy for you. Although they allow you to get thoughts out, it can be confusing deciding what to put in the center vs. the outlying circles. You would have to determine what is the main idea and what are your supporting details. You may want to skip this choice.

Some prewriting strategies that might be more effective include:

➤ Use a graphic organizer with built-in structure, such as a story map or sequence chart, rather than an open-ended one, such as a web.

➤ Use a software program that allows you to type in some key words and points and that will help you organize them at a later date (see Chapter 4).

➤ Don't worry about your handwriting or spelling when prewriting.

➤ Instead of sentences, use illustrations or computer graphics.

➤ In need of a topic? Start with your areas of passion or interest. Here is an opportunity to combine your assignment with something you already enjoy learning about! Still don't have any ideas? Stand in front of a bookshelf in the library and randomly point your finger at a book. Let yourself have three tries before picking one.

➤ Ask your teacher to give you three possible topics to write about instead of having endless possibilities.

➤ Ask your teacher for an outline of what is expected, sometimes called a rubric.

Now that you have done your prewriting tasks, and you have all of these ideas sitting on your paper, what are you going to do with them? Because you probably work better when you are clear about the rules, having a plan or rubric will help you cruise through this next part of the writing process. Step 2 of the writing process is composing a rough draft. This requires you to take all of your great ideas and somehow put them in a logical order that when read will make sense to the reader. The great part about this stage is that you don't have to worry about neatness, grammar, spelling, and other mechanics. Here is one strategy that can be very effective:

1. Take each key point from your prewriting stage and create one simple sentence with it on an index card.
2. Continue until all of your key points are mentioned.
3. Move the index cards around until they are in an order you believe is effective.
4. Either write or type your sentences in this order.

Other strategies to assist you in this drafting phase include:

➤ Use a software program, such as Inspiration, that allows you to create sentences based on picture icons and helps organize them into a coherent written piece.

➤ Use a paragraph organizer to help you remember the rules of constructing a paragraph. Some schools use a picture of a hamburger with the buns representing the topic sentence and concluding sentence and the meat, lettuce, and tomato representing the details.

➤ Make sure your teacher gives you an outline of what is expected from this assignment. If you are asked to write a letter, a model letter could be provided to you.

The next stage is editing and revising, which is just as it sounds. Remember to have a self-editing checklist when doing this. If your rough draft is already on the computer, you can check for spelling and grammar, but there is no checker to see if your writing makes sense to the reader. If your rough draft is by hand, use a self-editing checklist (see Figure 9) in order to edit your work. Your editing checklist can be customized to meet your needs and be unique to you, which is why it will work. You may not need to be reminded to capitalize the first word of each sentence or to end a sentence with a period, but you may need to be reminded not to write short sentences and to check your spelling.

My report has at least three paragraphs.	
Each paragraph has a topic sentence.	
Each paragraph has at least three supporting details.	
Each paragraph has a concluding sentence.	
All of my sentences begin with a capital letter.	
All of my sentences have punctuation.	
My report has a beginning, middle, and end.	
My report makes sense to the reader.	

Figure 9. Example of self-editing checklist for organization and content.

Other items on your checklist could include:
➤ Does it make sense when I read it to myself?
➤ Does it make sense to a different reader?
➤ Do my paragraphs all have a topic sentence, at least three supporting details, and a concluding sentence?
➤ Did the reader understand the purpose of my writing?
➤ Does my format match the teacher's expectations?

After editing, you will be writing your final draft and then publishing (which also means printing out in final draft form). Believe it or not, that's it!

AREA OF NEED 9: KEEPING UP WITH THE PACE OF THE CLASS

Let's look at all of the tasks you may need to do when you walk into a classroom. (Remember, this is just one class, there may be as many as six or seven more in your day depending on your school schedule).

1. Come into class
2. Put your homework in the designated place
3. Unpack backpack or notebook
4. Sit down at your seat
5. Take out planner, textbook, notebook, and pencil
6. Copy homework into planner
7. Open your book to the correct page
8. Pick up your pencil off the floor (if you've dropped it)
9. The list continues . . .

It is overwhelming just seeing it in writing. What happens if while you are picking up your pencil, the teacher tells everyone to turn to page 95? You sit up and listen to your teacher's lecture and have no clue what she is talking about. Your book is still open to page 45 and it does not match the classroom. A neurotypical student would instinctively look over at his neighbor's book and realize that he was on the wrong page. You might not think to do this. What are some strategies you could use?

Strategies to maintain the pace of the class:

➤ Know the routine, plan ahead.
➤ If the teacher gives the class 5 minutes for independent reading, set your watch timer to 4 minutes so when it beeps, you know you will have one more minute to finish.
➤ Write the routines down in the front of your binder for that class so if you forget where to turn an assignment in, you can refer to your chart.
➤ During class, if you can't find the page, ask a neighbor or just take a quick peek over his shoulder. He will probably not even know you are there.
➤ Before getting more lost, take a breath and raise your hand and ask the teacher where you are. It's really not as scary or embarrassing as you imagine.

AREA OF NEED 10: MULTITASKING

What is all the fuss about multitasking? You can watch television while you eat your cereal in the morning, right? How hard is it, really, to do two things at once? VERY!

Mallory, a 16-year-old student with NLD, was sitting in biology lab trying to copy the notes from the board while her teacher was explaining what their lab was about that day. Do you think Mallory . . .

A. Copied all of the notes down and understood the lab for the day?
B. Finished copying the notes?
C. Copied some of the notes from the board and heard some information about the day's lab?

It would probably be safe to say that the answer would be "C." She was able to do some copying and some listening, but neither would be effective and that would be evident on her next quiz. Instead, your plan of attack can be to:

➤ Let your teacher know that you cannot copy notes at the same time as listening to him lecture. Ask him to provide copies of his lectures so you can focus on just listening to him speak.
➤ Tape-record the class for later use.
➤ Ask a friend that you trust for a copy of his or her notes.

AREA OF NEED 11: STAYING RELAXED AT SCHOOL

No, that is not a joke. There are actual ways for you to stay relaxed and calm at school. Do you remember what 13-year-old Chris said in the beginning of this chapter when asked to describe his most difficult part of his day? He said, "The most difficult part of my school day is getting there because it's the early morning and you have to readjust to being there." Chris arrives at school feeling stressed simply from the transition. When you are feeling anxious, there are some things you can do to help you calm yourself. These include:

➤ Find a trusted adult or peer to talk to.
➤ Listen to an iPod (if permitted).

➤ Find a quiet space in the building. Always let an adult know where you are going.

➤ Get some exercise and drink water.

➤ Take a break.

➤ Breathe deeply to promote calm.

➤ Do Tai Chi, yoga, or other movement to alleviate stress.

Wrap Up: Tips and Tricks for Classroom Success

➤ **Learn when a strategy, or plan of attack, is needed.** Strategies can be used to help in areas where you are challenged. The most effective strategies let you use your areas of strength to compensate for your areas of need.

➤ **Learn how to work with classroom systems.** Learn procedures for each class, that is, the basic information for how to operate within that setting. Classroom procedures include where you sit and how you select your seat, when and how to turn in assignments, what materials you need to bring with you, classroom expectations, and lesson plans.

➤ **Use effective strategies to stay organized.** Decide what the most effective way is for you to keep your binder, whether you need one notebook or two, and how to keep track of papers and supplies. Remember to consider assistive technology options, as well as to use the calendar system you learned in Chapter 5.

➤ **Have a plan for working in a group.** Consider asking the teacher to allow you to work with students you already know and trust. When you are assigned to a group, take a few minutes together to decide who is responsible for what parts of the assignments. Volunteer for a position in the group that uses your areas of strength.

➤ **Use strategies to help with note-taking.** See if you can get a copy of the teacher's notes or notes from another student. Ask the teacher if you can tape-record the lecture. Use assistive technology options.

➤ **Use test-taking strategies to improve your score.** There are tips and tricks for test-taking skills in general, as well as specific strategies to use for multiple-choice tests or essay questions.

➤ **Different strategies can help you with math, depending on your needs and learning style.** Do you learn better when someone explains something to you with words or by looking at charts and pictures? Would you learn your math facts better with a program that puts them to music you can sing along to or by quizzing yourself with flash cards? There are effective strategies to help learn math skills that use each of these areas. Decide which is your strength and go from there.

➤ **Use strategies to help with reading comprehension.** Chances are you are pretty good at reading. However, there is more to reading than being able to decode the words. Reading comprehension is not only

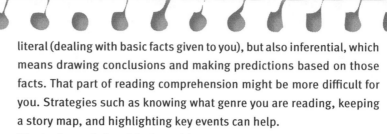

literal (dealing with basic facts given to you), but also inferential, which means drawing conclusions and making predictions based on those facts. That part of reading comprehension might be more difficult for you. Strategies such as knowing what genre you are reading, keeping a story map, and highlighting key events can help.

➤ **Strategies to help with the writing process.** Determine the purpose of your writing assignment. Remember FAT-P: **F**orm—Are you writing a letter, essay, advertisement, or poem? **A**udience—Who is your audience? If you are writing a letter, who do you expect to be reading it? **T**opic—What is the main idea? **P**urpose—Are you writing to inform, to persuade, or to express personal ideas? Use a variety of strategies to assist with the phases of writing: prewriting or generating ideas, drafting, editing, and revising.

➤ **Be aware of ways to keep up with the pace of the class.** Know the routine ahead of time. Use time management strategies. If you fall behind or become confused, don't be afraid to ask the teacher or a neighbor. It's better than becoming completely lost!

➤ **Use strategies to address times when you are expected to multitask.** It's hard to do several things at once. Work out strategies with your teacher in advance to find ways to accomplish one task at a time.

➤ **Use strategies to stay relaxed at school.** When things become overwhelming, take some time out to talk things over with a teacher, counselor, or friend. Take a break, even if it's just to get a drink of water, and remove yourself briefly from the source of stress and regroup. Use deep breathing, yoga, or other techniques to help your body relax.

CHAPTER 7

HOW IMPORTANT ARE APPEARANCE AND GOOD HYGIENE?

MISSION:

To understand why appearance and good hygiene are important and make them part of your daily routine.

When asked whether or not appearance and good hygiene mattered to them, three boys with Asperger's syndrome and/or Nonverbal Learning Disorder each had a different take on the subject.

Brian, age 10: "I don't care how clean people are. They're not my family."

Alex, age 14: "Appearance? I don't really care about this. I've got OCD, though, and hygiene and health are REALLY important to me. So, you can see, these can be different."

Steve, age 16: "People should be neat and presentable because it shows that they want to succeed, and one of the ways to do this is to dress well and to be neat."

> **Does appearance and good hygiene matter to you?**

> "Appearance? I don't really care about this."

Whose point of view do you agree with? If you agree with Steve, and good hygiene and a neat appearance are already part of your daily routine, then you can probably skip this chapter. If you are someone who doesn't believe that appearance and good hygiene are important enough to pay attention to, it is probably for one of two reasons. The first reason has to do with your general attitude. Just like Brian, you might not care about how clean other people are, and might not think they should notice or care about you.

The second reason is more physical in nature, and has to do with sensory integration and motor skills. Sometimes people with AS or NLD can be very sensitive to smell, taste, touch, or texture. These are called **sensory issues**. It might be truly uncomfortable to brush your teeth or comb your hair, and so these might be tasks that you'd rather just skip. You have learned that having AS or NLD affects your fine motor skills, which

> **sensory issues:** when your brain does not correctly use information about sights, sounds, textures, smells, tastes, and movement

are movements that require a high degree of control or precision, like handwriting. So, for the same reasons that handwriting can be a difficult task, tying shoes and manipulating dental floss also can be hard for you. Fortunately, there are strategies to help you understand both the how and the why of good hygiene, and to work around some of these sensory and motor issues.

WHY IT MATTERS

If you think hygiene and appearance don't say anything about what kind of person you are inside, think again. A neat appearance is a sign that you respect and take care of yourself. First impressions count for a lot in the neurotypical world.

As you learned in Chapter 2, having AS or NLD makes you a little different from your NT peers, and can mean that you stand out in many ways. Some of the differences in the way you think and respond can make you stand out in a good way. Others can cause difficulty getting along. This is one of those areas. People are not going to want to be with a person who does not smell clean or has poor hygiene. By recognizing and addressing this issue, you are taking control of the image you present to others.

➤ Whether or not you think it is important, people you come into contact with will form their first impressions of you based on whether you are neat and clean. This doesn't mean you have to keep up with the latest fashions, or even tuck in your shirt all of the time, but it does mean that your clothes should match, fit reasonably well, and be clean.

➤ Your overall hygiene is important. Your hair doesn't need to be short if you're a boy, or styled if you're a girl, but it does need to be clean and combed. Your face should be clean, your teeth brushed and flossed, and your body should smell pleasant or have no odor at all.

Good hygiene is important for more than just appearance's sake. It is important for your health.

> ➤ Washing your hands before eating or after coming in from outside can reduce your risk of catching colds or other surface-based viruses or bacteria.
> ➤ Brushing and flossing your teeth will prevent cavities or problems with your gums.
> ➤ Washing your hair frequently improves its health.

So if you didn't think it mattered whether or not you take care of yourself, now you should. Hopefully you are beginning to see that appearance and hygiene are not just about what others think of you, they also are about what *you* think of you.

What happens when you know why good hygiene and a neat appearance are important, but sensory and motor issues get in the way of making this part of your daily routine?

WORK AROUND SENSORY AND MOTOR ISSUES

If you are already working with an occupational therapist, then you know that this is a person who can teach you ways to compensate for or work around sensory-based difficulties. There also are a number of books written just for that purpose, and some helpful resources are listed at the end of this book.

It may be frustrating that a task like getting dressed may require strategies and work-arounds. You are not the only one who has challenges in this area. You are in good company—just ask actor Daniel Radcliffe, famous for playing Harry Potter in the movies. In August 2008, he revealed in an interview with the U.K.'s *Daily Mail* that he has **dyspraxia**, a neurological condition that affects motor skills. At age 19, Radcliffe still has difficulty tying his shoes and writing neatly. That certainly hasn't stopped him from succeeding!

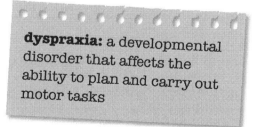

dyspraxia: a developmental disorder that affects the ability to plan and carry out motor tasks

The next time someone tells you that it's taking too long to tie your shoes, you can say, "What's the big deal? Harry Potter has the same problem." In the meantime, here are some tips and tricks to help with some of the most common sensory issues that interfere with neat appearance and good hygiene.

WEAR USER-FRIENDLY CLOTHES

Sometimes getting dressed in the morning can feel like a battle. Buttons on jeans may be tricky to button, and you may not have enough strength in your fingers to easily snap snaps. Shoes can take so long to tie, if you can even get them tied right at all. Tags on clothing can leave you itchy and sore all day. Fortunately, there are many options in clothing that can make these daily struggles unnecessary.

Look for pull-on pants with elastic, comfort, or even drawstring waistbands. The Lands End Company, for example, allows you to shop for pants online sorted by type of waistband. Pull-on skirts or dresses may be more comfortable options for girls than jeans or other pants. Many shirts and undergarments are now available "tagless" for extra comfort. As for shoes, slip-on shoes, twist-up laces, or Velcro® close sneakers can make a world of difference. Many popular shoe companies make such shoes, so you don't necessarily have to sacrifice style for comfort, if that's a concern.

LAY OUT YOUR CLOTHES THE NIGHT BEFORE

In addition to making sure that your clothes are user-friendly, choosing what you are going to wear and laying it out before you go to sleep gives you more time in the morning to spend on other tasks.

TRY AN ELECTRIC TOOTHBRUSH OR FLOSS PICK

Oral sensitivity can sometimes interfere with good oral hygiene. This means that sometimes it doesn't feel good when you put a toothbrush in your mouth. It may even make you feel like you want to gag. Many people find that an electric toothbrush is easier to tolerate. Sometimes the taste of toothpaste can be a problem. Fifteen-year-old John, for instance, hates the taste of mint. Luckily, he has been able to find vanilla- and citrus-flavored toothpastes.

Flossing also can be difficult, on two fronts. Just like with brushing, if you have oral sensitivities, flossing may feel very uncomfortable. Flossing also can be affected by fine motor skills. It may be hard to grip the floss correctly, or manipulate it with your hands to get between your teeth. One possible solution is to try floss picks instead of traditional dental floss. Floss picks are made by a variety of companies, and are available in drugstores and supermarkets near the toothpaste. A floss pick is a small, disposable, Y-shaped tool that holds a bit of floss across the top of the Y. It is much easier to use and guide between your teeth than traditional dental floss. Some companies even manufacture kid's versions with fun flavors like bubble gum.

TAKE A BATH INSTEAD OF A SHOWER

Sometimes showering may feel prickly for those with AS or NLD, and a bath may be a better option. Remember when filling the tub to find a temperature that is comfortable for your body. Baths may have challenges too. The temperate change from getting into the bath and then getting out and putting on new clothes or pajamas present a different kind of sensory issue. One way to reduce that is to bring your clothes into the bathroom and have your towel ready. You have to decide which method works best for you.

EXPERIMENT WITH FOAMING SOAPS AND WASHCLOTHS

Bethany, age 11, never liked the feeling of water on her face. She wouldn't put her face underwater when swimming, and she didn't like to wash her face in the sink. But she found that she didn't mind a warm, wet washcloth as much. Using foaming soap, which she then wiped off with the washcloth, enabled her to keep her face clean in a way that was more comfortable for her.

TRY UNSCENTED DEODORANT

Strong scents, even perfumes, may be unpleasant to you if you are overly sensitive to smells, and you might be tempted not to use any deodorant for this reason. Many deodorants are available without an added scent, and can keep you smelling fresh without irritating you with perfumes.

USE AN ELECTRIC RAZOR INSTEAD OF A STRAIGHT BLADE

If you shave, whether it be your face, legs, or underarms, and you have difficulty with fine motor skills like handwriting or cutting with scissors, chances are you may have difficulty controlling a razor blade as well. An easy way to avoid nicks and cuts is to use an electric razor instead.

These are some of the more common workarounds for many of the sensory and motor issues that impact grooming and hygiene. Give them a try, and see if they make your morning or evening routine a little easier.

INCORPORATE NEATNESS AND HYGIENE INTO YOUR DAILY ROUTINE

Just like the charts you learned about in Chapter 5 that help manage your time and homework strategies, you can create systems to help you with your hygiene routines. Being proactive by setting schedules and learning how to self-monitor is crucial in this area. Now let's create a plan of attack. You will use the charts in Figures 10 and 11 to create a method to begin your morning routine.

On the first chart (Figure 10), list all of your morning health and hygiene activities.

1. Working your way down, write a list of all of the personal care and hygiene routines you feel are key. Put the list in order of which one you will do first, then second, and so on.
2. Estimate how much time it should take you to complete each task. You should estimate on the higher end. For example, if you say brushing your teeth takes 2 minutes, make it 3. If you think showering takes 5 minutes, make it 6 or 7. Give yourself some leeway (see the example in Figure 10).
3. Total the number of minutes for the tasks to be completed.

Sample Chart

Task	Estimated Time
Brush teeth	4 minutes
Take a shower	10 minutes
Brush/Dry hair	5 minutes: boy 10 minutes: girl
Get dressed	5 minutes
Eat breakfast	10 minutes
Total:	34 minutes for a boy 39 minutes for a girl

Blank Chart

Task	Estimated Time

Figure 10. Hygiene routine charts.

Now let's figure out your wake-up time in order to fill out the second chart in Figure 11 and create a schedule.

1. On the bottom line of the chart, fill out the time that you need to leave for school.
2. Take the total number of minutes required to complete your morning routine from the first chart, and subtract this from the time you need to leave for school. Add 10 minutes and that will give you your wake-up time.
3. Now fill in the chart by listing in order each activity you need to do. For example, the chart in Figure 10 lists brushing your teeth as the first activity. Continue this process.
4. Make adjustments as necessary.

You will need to self-monitor this task and adjust times and/or tasks as needed. You also may want to include transition times between activities in your schedule. When you have developed your schedule, you can post it on your bathroom mirror as a reminder.

Sample Chart

Time	Task
6:50	Wake-Up/Snooze
7:00	Brush teeth
7:05	Shower
7:15	Get dressed
7:20	Brush/dry hair
7:25	Eat breakfast
7:35	Leave for school

Blank Chart

Time	Task

Figure 11. Create your morning schedule.

Wrap Up: Tips and Tricks for Maintaining Good Hygiene

➢ **Understand why it matters.** Appearance and good hygiene are important not only to how others perceive you, but also to maintain good health.

➢ **Work around sensory and motor issues that get in the way of maintaining good hygiene and a neat appearance.** Stick to easy-to-fasten clothes; use an electric toothbrush and an electric razor; use floss picks instead of traditional dental floss; use washcloths and foaming soaps if you don't like the feel of water on your face; or apply unscented deodorant if you are bothered by smells.

➢ **Develop an organizational system that reminds you to practice good hygiene and allows you sufficient time for your morning routine.** Use the chart system to list your activities and create a morning routine. You can post your chart on your bathroom mirror as a reminder.

CHAPTER 8

UNDERSTANDING FRIENDSHIP

What's It All About?

MISSION:
To develop strategies for being a good friend and to think about your friend's point of view.

F riendships can be complicated. Just when you think you've got someone figured out, she turns around and does something you didn't expect. Or, your reaction might not be what she expected. Back in the first chapter, 16-year-old Travis said that part of Asperger's syndrome is that "nobody can understand, nor can they tell what the Asperger person is really feeling." You may be surprised to learn that with the right strategies and effective self-advocacy, it is possible for NT friends to understand you. You can even learn to decode their behavior by paying attention to both their words and their body language and by using information-gathering techniques.

A group of students with AS and NLD described the top three qualities they looked for in a friend. You can see that the same qualities made just about everybody's list:

Travis, age 16: "same likings, willing to come over, someone who wouldn't abandon me"

Alex, age 14: "funny, nice, understanding"

Sean, age 17: "nice, smart, funny"

Brian, age 10: "positivity, nonviolence, happy"

Bill age 15: "intelligence, likability, common interests"

Steve, age 16: "dependability, intelligence, kindness"

Mark, age 15: "honesty, able to talk at my level, nice"

Amy, age 15: "nice, caring, honest"

> **What are the top three qualities you look for in a friend?**

> "nice, caring, honest"

When asked about what might make them angry with a friend, these students also had similar opinions:

Travis, age 16: "If they are mean to me"

Sean, age 17: "mean people, teasing, stealing"

Brian, age 10: "fighting and arguing, or making fun"

Steve, age 16: "being blown off, major disagreements, insults"

Mark, age 15: "talking about me behind my back, lying"

> **What would make you angry with a friend?**

> "If they are mean to me."

Sounds like friendship can be pretty black and white, right? You're nice or you're mean; you're honest or you are a liar. Not really. So much of understanding friendship comes down to communication, both words and body language, giving people the benefit of the doubt (which means believing that, sometimes, friends will do things that upset you without meaning to and without realizing it), and taking risks. This means different things at different ages, as you will see from these examples below.

YOU CAN'T READ THEIR MINDS, AND THEY CAN'T READ YOURS

Let's revisit Max from Chapter 2. Max was the student who, upon learning that he had NLD, talked about it in terms of not being able to find the right CD-ROM in his brain to answer questions quickly enough. Like most everyone with NLD, or AS for that matter, Max also had trouble making friends. He wanted to be included, but he felt alone on the playground at recess. Nobody wanted to play the games he liked, and when kids did ask him to play with him, it was usually something Max thought was dumb, like four square. That made Max angry. Didn't they know that he hated four square?

The other kids couldn't understand why Max would get so angry when they asked him to join their games. Max saw the situation differently. He genuinely thought everybody knew how much he hated four square, and that the only reason they asked him to play was to annoy him! Or, he thought, maybe they were asking because they knew he'd say no, and that way they didn't have to play with him at all. What kind of friends were these?

When you stop and think about it, did all of Max's classmates really know that he hated four square? Even if he and his classmates had talked about it once or twice, they still might not remember. They can't read Max's mind and just as importantly, Max can't read their minds. He can't know for sure if they really didn't want to play with him. Instead of getting angry, here are some strategies that Max could use to get what he wants—to play a game with his classmates that all of them will enjoy:

➤ Max could answer honestly, "I don't really like four square all that much, is there something else we could play?"

➤ Max could ask if they could take turns, maybe play four square for 15 minutes, and then play something that he chooses for another 15 minutes.

➤ Max could try to see if there was a way to participate with his friends without actually playing. Could he keep score, or be the referee?

➤ Finally, choosing not to play is an option, but with the understanding that no harm was meant in asking. Maybe he can play something else with them another time, when they are playing something he likes better.

Can you think of other strategies that might work for you?

FRIENDSHIP ISN'T ALL OR NOTHING

Erin, age 12 and diagnosed with AS, has vowed never to speak to Delia again. She trusted Delia with a secret. Delia told Susan, and before long the whole class knew. How could Delia betray her like that? Erin didn't care how many times Delia said she was sorry. A friend should keep a secret. So how could she ever think of Delia as a friend again?

Erin's example is a little more complicated, and something that most people struggle with at one time or another regardless of whether or not they have AS or NLD. We have high expectations of our friends, and sometimes they let us down. In Erin's case, she trusted Delia with a secret, and Delia broke that trust. Does this mean that she is no longer a friend?

Friendship isn't all or nothing. In other words, there are levels between being a friend and being an enemy. There also are different categories of friends. An acquaintance, for example, is someone who seems friendly but who you don't know very well. A classmate can be a friend in school, but you may not see her outside of the school setting. Then there are close friends who you can tell everything and trust with all of your secrets. Those friends are special and rare. There also are close friends you can still have fun with, but who you know can't resist passing on juicy gossip.

Erin has a choice to make. She needs to think about what qualities Delia brings to their friendship, and whether those good qualities are enough to outweigh the bad ones, including how she broke Erin's trust. If Delia feels really bad and has apologized, should Erin give her another chance? Here are some of the choices to consider:

➤ Erin can decide that telling her secret was too important and too upsetting, and she can't continue her friendship with Delia.

➤ Erin could go to the other extreme, and forgive Delia and resume the friendship as it was before.

➤ Erin can tell Delia that she'd like to stay friends, but that it's important for her to know that she can trust Delia in the future, and ask Delia whether she can count on her to keep a secret in the future.

➤ Erin can decide that there are some fun things that she can continue to do with Delia, but from now on she just won't tell her any secrets that she doesn't want people to know.

Which response would you choose? There is no "right" answer, the important thing is to understand that there are other ways to handle this situation besides **all**, which would mean remaining the closest of friends without any consequences, or **nothing**, which would mean not being friends anymore. You probably can think of even more choices that aren't listed. This is how most NT's manage their friendships, although they may not even be aware that they're doing it. There are some friends you hang out and play video games with; some friends you go to the mall with; some friends whose shoulders you cry on when you need some comfort; and some friends who you only talk to in class. We all have our flaws, and we all have our limits. Part of being a friend is accepting those flaws and limits in other people, as long as there are still enough good qualities there to make the friendship worthwhile. After all, isn't that how you would want someone to treat you?

TAKE A RISK, TRY SOMETHING NEW

John, a 15-year-old high school freshman diagnosed with NLD, hung up the phone with his friend Eric and wondered what to do. Eric called him on a Friday night, and asked if he wanted to be the fourth man on his team in a video game tournament the next day at a store across town. John always wanted to play in a video game tournament, but he quickly said no. So many things could go wrong! He had never been to the store that was holding the tournament, and he didn't know what to expect. He hadn't met Eric's other teammates, and he hadn't even played the latest version of the video game yet. He was afraid that if he messed up, or he became responsible for the team losing, that everyone would make fun of him. Maybe Eric wouldn't even want to be his friend anymore.

In John's situation, his fear of the unknown is getting in the way of something he'd really like to do. John read about video game tournaments in magazines and always thought they were really cool. He knew that his friend Eric had played in some tournaments, and they constantly discussed strategy, but when the opportunity arose to participate, John said no. Have you ever been torn between something you'd really like to try, and fear because you didn't know what to expect? Did this prevent you from getting together with a friend?

We all know that trying new things can be risky, but the rewards can be great. Sure, John might not do so well his first time out, but he will have gained experience and taken the first step toward something that he always dreamed of doing. If fear of the unknown is making you hesitate, then one strategy to pursue is to try to get more information before making a final decision. There are several ways to approach this:

➤ John could call Eric back and ask him to provide more details about the tournament. What is the store like? How does it work? What will happen when they arrive, and what is it like to play?

➤ John also was afraid of what would happen if he messed up. He can discuss that with Eric, too. He can ask, "Is the team really good? Will they get mad at me if I mess up?" John might find out that the rest of the team has no more experience than he does. Or he might find out that they're very competitive. Either way, that would be a key piece of information to help in the decision-making process.

➤ John can ask Eric why he was being invited, so that he's clear about his friend's expectations. Was John invited because of his "mad skills?" Was it because Eric knew that John had an interest in tournaments? Or was it maybe because they needed four people in order to enter the tournament, and they couldn't find a fourth? Believe it or not, that's not necessarily a bad thing, and might even take some of the pressure off. If they are desperately looking for a fourth teammate, the team knows that no matter how well or poorly John plays, they wouldn't be able to participate at all if he didn't come!

Ultimately, the decision whether to accept the invitation and enter the video game tournament with Eric's team is up to John. Taking a risk and trying something new is scary. Gathering more information can ease some of those fears, and help to make an informed decision about whether to socialize with friends, instead of a blind one based only on fear. What would you do in John's situation? Would you stay home, or would you take a chance and go?

LEARN THE SECRET CODE

All of the examples above are situations where direct communication can help you to understand what is going on in a friendship, and decide what to do about it. But what about the times when communication isn't so direct? Body language is another form of communication. It also is

nonverbal communication: the use of facial expressions, gestures, eye contact, and body language to communicate a message to another person called **nonverbal communication,** or sending a message without using words. The problem is, people with AS or NLD have a lot of difficulty noticing or understanding nonverbal communication.

A person's gestures, facial expressions, and tone of voice can send a message or can even change the meaning of the words that she is saying. In fact, if the words that someone is saying don't seem to match up with her tone or gestures, then that is a signal that the tone or gestures are what you should be paying attention to. It's almost like learning a secret code.

How, for example, do you know when it's time to change the subject of a conversation? If the person you're talking to doesn't come out and say, "I've heard enough about dinosaurs," then how are you supposed to know that your favorite topic is beginning to bore him? Look for the secret code. Is your friend:

➤ Looking down at his watch repeatedly, or looking away from you more than once?

➤ Shifting his weight from one foot to another?

➤ Crossing his arms over his chest?

➤ Shrugging his shoulders instead of answering your questions?

These are just some of the nonverbal cues that signal when a person has lost interest. Watching for these cues and adjusting your conversation appropriately is an essential skill for making and keeping friends.

You might be asking yourself, why would anyone want to communicate this way at all? Why not just come out and say exactly what you mean? Remember why you're using this strategy guide— to figure out the tips, tricks, and unwritten rules that will help you succeed. Learning to understand body language in everyday communication is almost like learning a cheat code for a video game. Once you figure it out, it helps you to better understand what people mean.

It also is important to pay attention to body language and tone of voice when you're trying to figure out if someone is teasing you in a mean way or in a friendly way. If someone you are playing a game with says, "You're such a nerd!" he might be saying it to be mean to you, or he might be teasing you in a friendly way. How do you know the difference? If he says it with a smile on his face, or a dismissive wave of the arm, or gives a little chuckle, these are the nonverbal signals to indicate that chances are he's joking around with you. You may not like that, and you can even tell him so, although not in an angry way: "Hey, Bill, I really don't like it when you say that, OK?" On the other hand, if his voice is loud and harsh, if his eyes are narrowly slit when he's looking at you, if his arms are on his hips or he's shaking a finger at you, these are nonverbal indicators that it's more likely he's being mean. Although that's still not an excuse for you to yell or get super angry back, it can be a signal to you that this is not someone you want to hang around with.

Learning to be aware of nonverbal language takes a lot of practice. Fortunately, there are some fun ways to do that. Here are some strategies you can try at home:

➤ Watch your favorite television show with the sound muted. See if you can figure out what's going on from the actor's facial expressions and gestures. You can turn the sound back on to see if your guess was right. If your television set has closed captioning, you can turn that on and continue to watch without the sound and check the words on the bottom of the screen to see if you were able to guess correctly.

➤ Look for movies or television shows where one or more of the characters convey their thoughts and emotions with gestures instead of words. A great example is the British claymation series, "Wallace and Gromit." These movies and shorts feature a dog named Gromit, who speaks volumes without ever saying a word. They also are wildly funny!

➤ There also are DVDs created and books written specifically for the purpose of educating people on the autism spectrum, and others, about nonverbal communication. You can find some of these listed in the Resources section at the end of this book.

One very important unwritten rule is that there are times when just blurting out what you feel is considered rude (even if it's true). One way to get the message across without being blatantly rude can be with body language, as we just discussed. Another leads us to our next strategy.

SOMETIMES IT'S OK NOT TO TELL THE WHOLE TRUTH

Maybe you've heard the expression "little white lies." Surely you have been taught that a good person tells the truth and that lying is a bad thing to do. In fact, among the group of students with AS or NLD surveyed, lying made everyone's list of things that might make them angry with a friend. Sometimes it's just not that simple. Sometimes, telling the whole truth might hurt someone's feelings. Sometimes a little white lie, or a small fib or half-truth to spare someone's feelings or to be polite, is the right choice to make.

This is not for important, life-or-death situations, or times when someone might be hurt or in trouble. This is about little everyday situations. For example, say your friend just got a new haircut, and you think it looks terrible. When she asks you how she looks, what do you say? You might want to tell the truth, and tell her that it looks awful and she should get it fixed right away! You might even think that you would appreciate that kind of honesty if you were in that position.

Here's an important tip: You will find that the most common reaction to that kind of honesty will be hurt feelings. It might even make your friend angry. A little white lie would be to say that her hair looks fine, even when you really think it doesn't. Or if you just can't bring yourself to say that, you might try a half-truth, like, "It's a very interesting haircut!" You can even avoid giving your answer by asking another question, such as, "How do you like it? Is it easy to take care of?"

Little white lies can sometimes help you to save face, too. Let's say you were invited to a party, and you really don't like the person throwing it. You don't want to go, but you need to respond to the invitation. So what do you tell him? The truth would be, "I'm not sure why you invited me, I've never liked you, and I wouldn't feel comfortable at your party." A much better choice would be to tell him, "I'm sorry, I'm busy that night," even if you're not. That way, his feelings aren't hurt, and you don't come off as being mean or rude.

In general, it's OK to tell a little white lie, or not tell the whole truth, as long as:

➤ It will do no harm.

➤ It will make a friend feel better.

➤ It will save face or provide a graceful exit out of an awkward situation.

Wrap-Up: Tips and Tricks for Understanding Friendship

➤ **Understand that you can't read their minds and they can't read yours.** Don't assume that you know what your friends are thinking, and don't be afraid to tell them how you feel.

➤ **Remember that friendship is not all or nothing.** If a friend lets you down, it doesn't always mean that you can't be friends anymore.

➤ **Take a risk. Try something new.** Don't let fear of the unknown get in the way of having a good time with your friends.

➤ **Learn the secret code.** How someone says something and what body language he or she uses is just as important as what he or she is saying.

➤ **Realize that sometimes it's OK not to tell the whole truth.** A little white lie to spare friends' feelings can go a long way toward maintaining a friendship.

CHAPTER 9

PUTTING IT INTO PRACTICE

Where Do I Meet New Friends?

MISSION:

To find ways to meet people with similar interests and make new friends.

n the last chapter, we looked at some of the strategies needed to create and maintain a friendship. Now that you understand what makes a good friend and how to be a good friend in return, it's time to figure out where to make the connections, and how to meet new neurotypical (NT) friends as well as other kids with AS or NLD.

MEETING NT KIDS

You spend most of your day at school, so it makes sense that this is the first place to turn to for meeting friends. The problem is that making friends isn't simple for a student with AS or NLD. It's not really like those picture books in kindergarten, where a little kid walks up to a classmate and asks, "Will you be my friend?" People seem to pair off or cluster together, and sometimes it's hard to tell how or why. It can be even harder to figure out how to join in.

LOOK FOR COMMON INTERESTS

Chances are you have a special interest or talent that occupies a substantial amount of your time. You may have found that when you talk about your favorite subject, your classmates don't want to hear about it, or they may not relate to it because their interests may be different. It's important to recognize when you have talked enough about a topic and it's time to give someone else a turn. Another strategy is to seek out people who love the same things you do. Use those special interests and talents to find friends! You can start by choosing elective classes that showcase your interest. This is a way to give you daily access to other students who share those interests.

For example, Charlie, a ninth grader with NLD, really enjoyed his theater elective. Charlie didn't know anybody in the class all that well, but when the teacher put students together in groups to act out their favorite scenes from a movie, he impressed everyone with his memory for movie dialogue. Charlie had an amazing ability to recite his favorite scenes word-for-word, even imitating foreign accents.

An important part of this class was participating in discussions about theater, movies, and acting methods. The discussions often would continue in the hallway after class, and Charlie discovered that his classmates were really interested in what he had to say. That was a real boost to his self-esteem. Much to his surprise, 3 weeks into the school year, one of his classmates invited Charlie to a party. That made Charlie feel really good; his confidence soared. He usually had to work hard at making new friends, but in theater class, where he was in his comfort zone, there was an easy connection.

The key to this positive experience was sharing an interest. In another class, such as algebra, Charlie's talent for remembering movie scenes word-for-word would not be appreciated or appropriate to share. But if he had memorized pi to 36 places . . . well, that is another story!

When specific classes are required, as opposed to electives that you can choose, or when the subject matter isn't something that you are especially interested in, you will have to look a little harder to find common interests. You can do this in several ways:

Listen carefully when your classmates talk to you or to each other.

Do they mention video games you've played or TV shows you've seen? Are they having the same trouble with the homework that you had last night? The first step is to figure this out.

Use a "polite interrupter" to join in the conversation.

This step requires a little bit of patience. You might be tempted to immediately interrupt a conversation if you hear something that you want to respond to, but this isn't usually well-received. A better strategy would be to wait for a pause in the conversation, and then use a "polite interrupter" to join in the conversation. Some examples of polite interrupters are: "Excuse me, did I hear you talking about "Lost"? I love that show! Did you watch it last night?" or, "I thought I heard you say that you had trouble with problem #6 in the homework . . . I did, too, but I think I figured it out. Do you need help?"

Can you think of situations that you've been in where you wished you could join a conversation? Can you think of "polite interrupters" you might have used to get you started?

Finding classmates with common interests and talking with them about those shared interests is the first step on the path to friendship.

EXPLORE AFTERSCHOOL CLUBS

Afterschool clubs are another great way to meet other students who share common interests with you. Middle schools and high schools usually have a wide selection of clubs and activities to choose from, and new members usually are warmly welcomed. Sometimes the clubs will even meet during lunch. Elementary schools will sometimes offer clubs or special-interest classes after school. If they don't, there are always local community centers or other local organizations to investigate. Ask your parents to help you out. This worked out really well for Adam, a 15-year-old who has always been interested in trains. As Adam's mother described:

Adam became interested in trains as a very young child. It was always his favorite toy, his favorite book; we made a point of watching for train events. We learned that we had a train club nearby that was open to the public, so we started taking him there. Because he was only 8 years old at the time, a parent was required to attend along with him. So, he and his dad went every Friday night.

The train club has an elaborate model train setup. It is run by a four-man crew. The average age of the members is 55 to 60, and not all of them were thrilled to have kids there. Adam's dad helped to bridge some of this, and with Adam's motivating interest he learned very quickly.

Within 2 years, Adam and his dad were invited to become full members (you have to have a standing member sponsor you). Now 7 years later, at age 15, Adam is well respected and relied on by the other members. He is not only a member of the crew, but he is the youngest member ever to hold the position of dispatching. It is the most complex position, and there are only a dozen or so members who know how to do it.

Adam has developed a real sense of success with his experience with the train club. He knows that with hard work he can do anything he wants to do. He has learned that there are many different social circles out there, and how to manage in each one!

As you can see, hobbies and interests are an excellent place to start when looking for common ground to connect with others.

EXPLORE INDEPENDENT SPORTS

Most kids with AS or NLD do not feel comfortable in a team sports setting. You may remember from the first chapter that gross motor skills (physical activities like throwing a ball) and fine motor skills (precise physical tasks like tying shoes) are affected by AS and NLD. On the playing field, this can mean that you might be less athletic than your peers, or even clumsy and confused. The way in which you process information differently from your peers can also add to confusion in a team sports setting. Take the game of soccer as an example. You might find yourself so distracted and disoriented by the large number of players on the field, that you forget to which goal you are supposed to be kicking. Everyone's feet seem to be moving so fast and in so many changing directions that it might not even occur to you to try to get the ball away from another player. In the meantime, teammates are criticizing you for standing and waiting until the ball is kicked to you. No wonder the very idea of team sports can cause anxiety!

Don't be discouraged by this. There are many other sports that can fit your style. You might want to try activities that are more independent in nature. These include martial arts, horseback riding, golf, weight training, or any sport where the goal is physical activity at an independent pace. With the pressure of "in-the-moment" competition eliminated, it can be easier to relax, have fun, and even form friendships with other kids who like the same sports.

CONNECTING WITH OTHER KIDS WITH AS AND NLD

Friendships with peers can be satisfying in many ways, such as having someone to talk to or sharing a common interest, but sometimes the most satisfying relationships are with other kids who also are diagnosed with AS or NLD, and who have faced the same challenges and triumphs that you have. As mentioned in the Introduction, recent estimates suggest that as many as 1 in 91 kids are diagnosed with an autism spectrum disorder. How and where can you find them?

SOCIAL SKILLS GROUPS

Social skills groups are a good way to meet other kids who have trouble in the same areas that you do. The benefit of social skills groups is that they take place in structured settings with planned activities and a knowledgeable adult to guide you. Sometimes a school counselor or speech pathologist will lead a lunchtime social skills group right at your school. They may call it something else, like "Lunch Bunch" or "Friendship Group." What it will involve is a few select students who get together with the counselor once a week or so. You might play board games and practice skills like taking turns or being a good sport. You might simply talk about social problems you've been having and work together to come up with solutions. You also may do some role-playing together to help you understand different points of view, review social stories, or practice conversation skills in a safe, nonjudgmental environment.

Specialized therapists outside the school day also lead social skills groups and workshops. Your parents will need to be involved to find appropriate social skills groups in your area. Your job is to be open to the experience, and willing to accept constructive criticism to help you succeed in the world of NTs. Some social skills groups only focus on kids and teens on the autism spectrum. These provide not only an opportunity to practice social skills, but an opportunity to meet, befriend, and learn from other kids who see the world just like you do.

SPECIALIZED SUMMER CAMPS

Summertime can be a tough time of year to make new friends or stay connected with old friends. You are not in school where you can easily see people everyday, and kids around the neighborhood may be away on vacation or at summer camps. Did you know that special summer camps exist for kids with challenges too? There are camps with a focus on occupational therapy, where you will learn fun activities to help strengthen your motor skills. There are camps for kids who need support with social skills. There are also special interest camps that might coincide with your areas of strength, such as drama camp or robotics camp.

AUTREAT

Autreat is an annual conference put together by the Autism Network International advocacy group. It takes place each summer in Bradford, PA. The agenda, rules, and space are designed by people with autism, for people with autism. The goal and focus is on the positive aspects of living with autism. Within Autreat, there are supervised activity programs for children under 18. Autreat is designed to provide opportunities to connect with other people on the autism spectrum and develop contacts and advocacy skills in a sensory-friendly environment. More information can be found at http://www.autreat.com.

SUPPORT GROUPS

Support groups are groups of people who are all having difficulty in a common area who get together to discuss their problems and help each other with solutions. Support groups can be led by an individual trained in the specific area, or by a person who has had similar experience in that area. Support groups can meet in person or online. Unfortunately, most support groups for individuals with AS or NLD are geared toward adults. Some traditional groups are geared toward teens, and some online support groups also include teens and kids.

Be sure to check out the Resources section in the back of this book for more information on AS, NLD, and where to find support. Some resources to get you started in the meantime include:

➤ GRASP, The Global and Regional Asperger Syndrome Partnership, runs online and regional support groups for teens. You can find out more at http://www.grasp.org.

➤ LDOnline, an Internet support group for adults and parents, has a kid's zone where you can share original stories or your experiences. The majority of the stories focus on children's own struggles and triumphs with a variety of disabilities. Maybe you'll read something that sounds familiar! You can read or submit stories at http://www.ldonline.org/kidzone.

➤ Delphi Forums is an Internet message board site. They offer discussion boards on a variety of topics, from hobbies and interests, to those dedicated to Asperger's syndrome and Nonverbal Learning Disorder. Many of the discussion boards are for parents, but there are some for teens, too. You must be 13 years old to register. You can go to http://www.delphiforums.com and enter "Asperger's syndrome" or "Nonverbal Learning Disorder" in the search box.

➤ Wrong Planet is an online resource and community for autism and AS created by college students. Among its many online discussion boards, Wrong Planet includes areas specifically for kids and adolescents with AS or autism spectrum disorders. You can join in at http://www.wrongplanet.net.

➤ There also are resources for your parents or other adults in your life that explain more about how people with NLD and AS view the world. Two such sites are http://www.nldbprourke.ca for background on NLD and http://www.aspergersyndrome.org for information on AS.

Of course, before participating in any online discussions, there are some basic safety guidelines that you should be aware of. This brings us to our next section.

MEETING FRIENDS ONLINE

It can be fun and convenient to chat with friends online. Students with AS or NLD were asked what they liked about connecting with their friends online:

Bill, age 15: "I have an opportunity to re-read things, and I am less likely to misunderstand."

Amy, age 15: "Facebook is a good way to interact with friends."

Sean, age 17: "I like instant messaging best."

What do you like about connecting with friends online?

"I have an opportunity to re-read things, and I am less likely to misunderstand."

Making friends through Facebook, MySpace, or Internet chat rooms can be fun, but safety should always be on your mind. There are definitely advantages to communicating over the Internet. For one, you can take time to think about and plan out your response. You can't do this in face-to-face conversations, which sometimes move too quickly. You can look things up that you don't understand before writing a reply. You can even ask an adult or another friend for ideas or for help. Despite these benefits, communication via chat room, message board, IM, or e-mail also can be frustrating or even dangerous. These guidelines can help you navigate cyberspace safely.

What you see isn't always what you get.

You don't need to look past today's headlines to realize that all isn't what it seems on the Internet. Whether it's a scam promising to make you rich, a stranger of the opposite sex who takes a sudden interest in you on a social networking site, or even a supposed friend from school instant messaging you while you're doing your homework, always think twice when communicating in cyberspace.

You need to be especially cautious if you are communicating with someone that you haven't met in person. Even if someone tells you his or her name, where he or she lives, or sends you a picture, always remember that these things are very easy to fake. Also *never* give out your personal information, such as your full name, birthday, address, or what school you attend.

Even though you may be having a perfectly nice conversation, meeting someone over the Internet is just like meeting a stranger on the playground. You wouldn't give a stranger your cell phone number, would you? A good rule to remember is: *When in doubt, print it out*! If you have any doubts about a conversation that you're having via e-mail, IM, chat, or an Internet site, print it out and check with a parent, teacher, or another adult that you trust.

There are a number of websites that promote cyber safety, and can give you tips on how to surf smart. Here are just a few:

➤ The National Center for Missing and Exploited Children maintains websites designed to teach safe habits for surfing the Internet and using social networking sites. You can find tons of useful information as well as play games and take surveys at http://www.netsmartz.org, http://www.nctsmartzkids.org, and http://www.nstccns.org.

➤ One of the original sites dealing with Internet safety, as well as cell phone safety, is Safekids. This site also has important information about how to recognize the manipulation tactics of child predators, and links for teens with tips about socializing and blogging. Learn more at http://www.safekids.com and http://www.safeteens.com.

➤ Wired Kids, Inc. is a charity whose mission is to protect kids from cybercrime and abuse. They maintain a website with information and a report line so that you can "report bad sites, or get advice if you've found something online you don't know how to deal with," at http://www.wiredkids.org.

➤ The Business Software Alliance maintains the Cyber Treehouse, where you can find links to games, videos, and safe sites at http://www.cybertreehouse.com, which is part of http://www.playitcybersafe.com.

Think before hitting "reply." Sometimes things seem a little harsh presented in black and white. Just like in a face-to-face conversation, it might be tough to tell in writing when someone is being sarcastic, or thinks he is being funny but falls short of the mark. Emoticons, the small graphics that can be added after a line of text, can sometimes help. When something reads negatively, but there is a winking emoticon at the end of the sentence like so ;-), that's an easy signal that maybe you shouldn't take the comments all that seriously. What if there aren't any obvious signs? How do you respond?

As the guideline suggests, think before hitting that reply button. As Bill pointed out above, you have an opportunity to re-read, and really think about the comments and the person writing them. If it's someone you know, is this typical of the way they talk to you? If it's someone you don't know, is there maybe more than one meaning to what they've written? And finally, before responding in anger, you always have the option of sending a message that simply says, "I'm not sure what you meant by that. Can you clarify?" Or an even simple "Huh?"

We asked teens: "Have you ever had a misunderstanding when communicating by e-mail because you didn't check your reply?"

Amy, age 15: "In sixth grade, I was telling my friend about a teacher named Ms. Buck, but I accidentally typed a wrong letter and my friend thought I cursed at her. I called her and apologized. I should have read what I typed before sending the message to her."

Remember to take the opportunity to read over your own reply before sending it off. Is it very long? Think about how you might say the same thing in a shorter message. Do you come across as angry, or like you're lecturing? Maybe you want to re-work your answer so that the reader will understand what you mean without taking offense. Was the e-mail sent to more addresses than just yours? Make sure you double-check whether you are replying to one person, or hitting "reply all" to send your response to the entire group.

Wrap-Up: Tips and Tricks for Meeting New Friends

➤ **Look for common interests.** Sharing an interest in the same subject, hobby, or even television show can make it easier to start up a conversation with someone new. Use your specialized interests or talents as a source of inspiration to connect with others!

➤ **Explore clubs, both in school and in the community.** This is a great way to meet up with people who are already interested in the same things you are.

➤ **Explore independent sports.** Although team sports often can be frustrating, sports where you achieve fitness at your own pace, such as martial arts, golf, horseback riding, or weight training, can provide both an opportunity for creating healthy habits and making friends with shared interests.

➤ **Try a social skills group.** This is a way to practice friendship skills in a safe environment.

➤ **Look for a specialized summer camp.** Special camps can provide an opportunity to meet people who share your interests, or are looking for fun, low-stress ways to work through similar challenges.

➤ **Participate in specialized retreats.** Autreat is designed to promote opportunities for people on the autism spectrum to meet and interact in a positive and sensory-friendly environment.

➤ **Look for support groups.** Whether in person or online, support groups provide an opportunity to meet and interact with people who see the world just like you do, and struggle in similar areas.

➤ **Stay safe online. What you see isn't always what you get!** Meeting new friends online can be fun, but there are some basic precautions you should always take. Never give out personal information to someone you haven't met in real life. If something doesn't seem right, *when in doubt, print it out* and show it to a parent, teacher, or trusted adult.

➤ **Think before hitting "reply."** You can misunderstand the meaning behind a conversation online just like you sometimes do in real life. Take advantage of the fact that when you communicate online, you can reread and really think about your reply.

CHAPTER 10
MISSION LOG

MISSION:
To use your new strategies to continue the quest, and keep a record of your adventures.

WHAT COMES NEXT?

N ow that you've read this strategy guide, hopefully you have begun to think about challenges in a new way. You've realized that having AS or NLD is not only nothing to be afraid of, but you also have some pretty cool strengths and talents. For those areas that can be difficult, you've learned that you're not the only one who sometimes has trouble. More importantly, you've learned new tips and tricks to help you succeed. The next step is to apply these strategies to real-life situations. In this chapter, we have provided journal pages to keep track of your own personal missions and record the strategies you use. Who knows, *you* may be the next student with AS or NLD to be quoted in a book to help others!

CHECKLIST: ARE YOU USING YOUR TIPS AND TRICKS?

As you record your own challenges and the steps you use to problem-solve, here is a checklist of the tips and tricks from previous chapters. You can refer back to the list as you decide which strategies to use. You also can use the prompts on the list to go back and reread chapters that might be helpful in your mission.

SELF-ADVOCACY
- ❏ Did I explain my needs?
- ❏ Did I ask for help if I needed it?
- ❏ If this is a school-related issue, do I have an IEP, 504 Plan, or other special plan? Is the issue something that is addressed in my plan?
- ❏ Is this something I need to speak to my teacher about? Have I made a list of the things I want to say? Are the things on my list specific? Do I need to practice with another adult to help my self-confidence?
- ❏ Am I being bullied? Have I answered the questions in Chapter 3 to help figure out if this is friendly teasing or bullying?

❏ Have I tried proactive strategies to avoid opportunities for bullying, such as being aware of my surroundings and whether the area is supervised by adults, looking for other options, or making arrangements for supervision by an adult?

❏ Have I tried appropriate reactive strategies, such as calmly telling the bully to stop, trying a comeback line, or telling an adult about the situation?

❏ If this is a home-related issue, have I calmly explained myself instead of losing my temper?

ASSISTIVE TECHNOLOGY

❏ Is there a device or program that can help me meet my needs?

❏ Have I considered using a handheld device to keep track of my schedule? Do I know the pros and cons of using a handheld?

❏ Do I need something to help me keep track of time? Have I considered different types of timers, both visual and audible?

❏ Do I use a computer or word processor when I write? Am I good at keyboarding, or do I need to practice that skill?

❏ Have I investigated all of the software and online options that can help me in areas such as writing, reading comprehension, and math?

HOMEWORK

❏ Do I have an organized space where I do my homework? Are all of my supplies there, ready for me to use?

❏ Have I identified my strengths and weaknesses? Have I figured out which assignments will be easier and which will be harder? Have I figured out which assignments should I do first?

❏ Am I managing my time? Do I know how to use timers and other devices or strategies to estimate how long my homework will take?

❏ Have I created monthly and weekly calendars to keep track of my assignments and other commitments and developed a schedule for both homework and breaks?

❏ Do I remember to hand in my homework? Do I use a homework folder? Have I tried self-advocacy strategies to get the support of the teacher?

❏ Do I have trouble beginning a writing assignment? Have I considered graphic organizers or organizational software to help me get my thoughts down on paper?

CLASSROOM STRATEGIES

❏ Am I thinking about strategies that use my strengths to meet my needs?

❏ Am I following strategies to help me with the 11 key areas of challenge in the classroom? These include:

    ❏ Learning how to work with classroom systems

    ❏ Organizing materials

    ❏ Group activities

    ❏ Taking notes

    ❏ Taking tests

    ❏ Math

    ❏ Reading comprehension

    ❏ Writing

    ❏ Keeping up with the pace of the class

    ❏ Multitasking

    ❏ Staying relaxed at school

HYGIENE

❏ Do I understand why a neat appearance and healthy habits are important to maintain?

❏ Have I learned how to compensate for sensory or motor issues that might interfere with getting dressed or practicing good hygiene habits?

❏ Have I developed a schedule that reminds me what to do and allows sufficient time for my morning hygiene routine?

UNDERSTANDING FRIENDSHIP

❏ Am I expecting others to read my mind? Have I told them how I feel? Can I give them the benefit of the doubt?

❏ If a friend does something to make me angry or upset, have I thought about whether we can get over it and still be friends?

❏ Am I willing to take a risk and try something new with a friend? Can I gather more information to help with my fear of the unknown?

❏ Am I paying attention to nonverbal language, or body language, as well as the words someone is saying?

❏ Will I consider telling a "little white lie" or not telling the whole truth, if it will do no harm and spare someone's feelings?

MEETING NT AND OTHER AS/NLD FRIENDS

❏ Have I used my special interests or talents as a starting point to look for common interests with classmates or peers? Is there an elective class I can take that is in my area of strength or interest?

❏ Have I investigated school-based or community-based clubs in my areas of interest?

❏ Have I thought about independent, noncompetitive sports, such as golf, horseback riding, martial arts, or weight training, as a way to both stay healthy and connect with others who also enjoy these activities?

❏ Am I enrolled in a social skills group, where I can meet others who might have AS or NLD, or practice friendship skills?

❏ Have I tried a specialized summer camp in my areas of interest or need?

❏ Am I aware of special retreats designed for people on the autism spectrum to connect with one another?

❏ Have I considered support groups, either in person or online, to connect with others with AS or NLD?

❏ When participating in online groups or activities, do I know how to stay safe? Do I remember never to give out personal information, such as my full name, address, phone number, or school? If I'm unsure about whether something is appropriate, do I show an adult?

❏   Do I think things through before e-mailing or communicating electronically?

READY TO TAKE ON YOUR MISSIONS?

Now it's time to record your own personal "missions." Here's how to use the journal. Don't be afraid to add your own pages if you need more space.

1.   Next time you are facing a challenge, think of it as your mission. In the space provided, write down some notes, draw a picture, or utilize technology to tell what you hope to achieve.

2.   In the space marked "My Challenges," record the difficulties that you are having that are keeping you from accomplishing this goal.

3.   Refer back to the checklists above. Which tips and tricks might help you overcome these obstacles? Choose at least three (you can choose more). Try these strategies.

4.   What worked and what didn't? Keep a list, so you'll know what to do next time!

MISSION LOG

My Mission: _____

_____

_____

My Challenges: _____

_____

_____

Tips and Tricks (See Checklists):

1. _____

_____

2. _____

_____

3. _____

_____

What Worked and What Didn't: _____

_____

_____

_____

_____

MISSION LOG

My Mission: _____

_____

_____

My Challenges: _____

_____

_____

Tips and Tricks (See Checklists):

1. _____

_____

2. _____

_____

3. _____

_____

What Worked and What Didn't: _____

_____

_____

_____

_____

MISSION LOG

My Mission: _____

_____

_____

My Challenges: _____

_____

_____

Tips and Tricks (See Checklists):

1. _____

_____

2. _____

_____

3. _____

_____

What Worked and What Didn't: _____

_____

_____

_____

_____

MISSION LOG

My Mission: _____

_____

_____

My Challenges: _____

_____

_____

Tips and Tricks (See Checklists):

1. _____

_____

2. _____

_____

3. _____

_____

What Worked and What Didn't: _____

_____

_____

_____

_____

MISSION LOG

My Mission: _____

_____

_____

My Challenges: _____

_____

_____

Tips and Tricks (See Checklists):

1. _____

_____

2. _____

_____

3. _____

_____

What Worked and What Didn't: _____

_____

_____

_____

_____

MISSION LOG

My Mission: _____

_____

_____

My Challenges: _____

_____

_____

Tips and Tricks (See Checklists):

1. _____

_____

2. _____

_____

3. _____

_____

What Worked and What Didn't: _____

_____

_____

_____

_____

RESOURCES

Below is a list of resources to help further your understanding of the topics covered in this book.

UNDERSTANDING AS AND NLD

Carley, M. J. (2008) *Asperger's from the inside out: A supportive and practical guide for anyone with Asperger's syndrome.* New York, NY: Perigee Penguin Group.

    Michael John Carley was diagnosed with AS as an adult, and offers firsthand experience as well as advice and support. He now runs GRASP, The Global and Regional Asperger Syndrome Partnership.

Fast, Y. (2004). *Employment for individuals with Asperger syndrome or nonverbal learning disability: Stories and strategies.* London, England: Jessica Kingsley.

    A collection of experiences in the work world from individuals with AS or NLD, compiled by an author who herself has NLD.

Grandin, T. (2006). *Thinking in pictures: My life with autism* (Expanded ed.). New York, NY: Vintage Books.

Temple Grandin, who has autism, writes about her life experiences in this book.

Jackson, L. (2002). *Freaks, geeks and Asperger's syndrome: A user guide to adolescence*. London, England: Jessica Kingsley.

Luke Jackson has Asperger's syndrome, and wrote this book at age 13 to share his experiences with others who might be able to relate.

Whitney, R. V. (2008). *Nonverbal learning disorder: Understanding and coping with NLD and Asperger's—What parents and teachers need to know*. New York, NY: Perigee Penguin Group.

Although written for parents, Rondalyn Varney Whitney's book contains many anecdotes about her son, who is diagnosed with NLD.

Delphi Forums
http://www.delphiforums.com

Delphi Forums is an Internet message board site. It offers discussion boards on a variety of topics, from hobbies and interests, to those dedicated to Asperger's syndrome and Nonverbal Learning Disorder. Many of the discussion boards are for parents, but there are some for teens, too. You must be 13 years old to register. Type "Asperger's syndrome" or "Nonverbal Learning Disorder" in the search box to find the correct forums.

Global and Regional Asperger Syndrome Partnership
http://www.grasp.org

The Global and Regional Asperger Syndrome Partnership (GRASP) is an organization run by individuals with autism that focuses on the positive aspects of AS. GRASP runs online and regional support groups for teens.

LD Online
http://www.ldonline.org/kidzone

LDOnline, an Internet support group for adults and parents, has a kid's zone where you can share original stories or your experiences. The majority of the stories focus on students' own struggles and triumphs with a variety of disabilities.

Nonverbal Learning Disorders Association
http://www.nlda.org

Nonverbal Learning Disorders Association (NLDA) is a nonprofit research and support group focusing on Nonverbal Learning Disorder. Check out the website's Resource Center for lists of books, articles, and notes from past conferences.

NLD on the Web

http://www.nldontheweb.org

Maintained by author and NLD expert Pamela Tanguay, this site is a clearinghouse for the latest information on Nonverbal Learning Disorder.

Organization for Autism Research

http://www.researchautism.org

The Organization for Autism Research (OAR) is dedicated to furthering research and understanding of the autism spectrum, and has produced a DVD in cooperation with GRASP called "Understanding Asperger's Syndrome: A Professor's Guide." This downloadable video has students with AS explain what kinds of accommodations work for them. It can be viewed at http://www.researchautism.org/resources/AspergerDVDSeries.asp

Wrong Planet

http://www.wrongplanet.net

Wrong Planet is an online resource and community for autism and Asperger's created by college students. Among its many online discussion boards, Wrong Planet includes areas specifically for kids and adolescents with Asperger's or autism spectrum disorders.

SELF-ADVOCACY FOR INDIVIDUALS WITH AUTISM SPECTRUM DISORDERS

Autism Network International

http://www.autreat.com

Autism Network International (ANI) is an advocacy and informational group run by and for people with autism spectrum disorders. ANI sponsors an annual conference called Autreat, designed especially for the needs of people on the autism spectrum.

Autistic Self Advocacy Network

http://www.autisticadvocacy.org

ASAN was founded and is run entirely by young adults with autism spectrum disorders. The organization promotes advocacy and inclusion and gives a voice in the national discussion about autism to those with autism spectrum disorders.

STRATEGIES TO COMBAT BULLYING

Dubin, N. (2007). *Asperger syndrome and bullying: Strategies and solutions.* London, England: Jessica Kingsley.

Nick Dubin is an adult with Asperger's syndrome who reflects back on how he was bullied in school and offers advice about what families and schools can do to combat bullying.

SPECIAL EDUCATION ADVOCACY, IEPS, AND 504 PLANS

Weinfeld, R., & Davis, M. (2008). *Special needs advocacy resource book: What you can do now to advocate for your exceptional child's education.* Waco, TX: Prufrock Press.

This book offers a comprehensive overview of the special education process, outlining not only your legal rights, but effective strategies to pursue them.

Wright, P., & Wright, P. (2006). *From emotions to advocacy: The special education survival guide* (2nd ed.). Hartfield, VA: Harbor House Law Press.

This book, along with its accompanying website below (Wrightslaw), explains the special education process and special education law, and offers advice for parents on how to advocate for their special needs children without becoming overly emotional.

Wright, P. W. D., & Wright, P. D. (2007). *Special education law* (2nd ed.). Hartfield, VA: Harbor House Law Press.

This book provides the actual text of the laws pertaining to special education, including the Individuals with Disabilities Act of 2004 (IDEA), Section 504 of the Rehabilitation Act of 1973, No Child Left Behind Act of 2001, Family Education Rights and Privacy Act, and McKinney-Vento Homeless Assistance Act. It also gives case law examples.

Wrightslaw
http://www.wrightslaw.com

This site accompanies the two Wrightslaw books above, offering excerpts, resources for families, and a searchable database for special education issues and laws.

ASSISTIVE TECHNOLOGY: PERSONAL DIGITAL ASSISTANTS

iPod touch
http://www.apple.com/ipodtouch

Apple's iPod touch is like a portable computer and personal organizer. You also can download a wide variety of applications, many of which are free, that can offer you access to different educational resources.

Palm T/X, PalmOne Zire
http://store.palm.com

The Palm T/X and PalmOne Zire are handheld devices that include a word processor, calendar, and built in Wi-Fi and Bluetooth. A sync feature allows you to store your information both on your handheld and on your personal computer.

ASSISTIVE TECHNOLOGY: TIME MANAGEMENT

WatchMinder
http://www.watchminder.com

This product is a programmable watch that both vibrates and displays messages.

Timex Tween Digital
http://www.timex.com/Timex-Tween-Digital/dp/B000MAXWJY

This cool watch has an audible alarm and clips on to your backpack or belt. This is also a good option if you are bothered by the sensation of wearing a wrist watch.

Online Stopwatch
http://online-stopwatch.com

This is a program to download to your computer. It will count up or count down, and you can create your own personal signals, such as a bell or applause, to let you know when time's up.

Time Timer
http://www.timetimer.com

This company makes both a wristwatch and a downloadable program for your personal computer. It is a visual timer featuring a red disc that shrinks as time passes. It comes in different sizes, and there is an optional audible feature.

Time Tracker® Visual Timer and Clock

http://www.learningresources.com

Type the product name into the Learning Resources® site to locate this item. This timer device works almost like a stoplight with green, yellow, and red indicators, alerting you to the amount of time you have remaining.

TimeTracker v2.0

http://formassembly.com/time-tracker/#

This product keeps track of any time you spend on a task, like a to-do list with a timer. Another version, TimeTracker 1.2.4., is a Firefox add-on that keeps track of how much browsing and surfing you do when on your computer for another reason, along with a "get back to work" alarm.

ASSISTIVE TECHNOLOGY: PORTABLE WORD PROCESSORS

NEO and DANA

http://www.neo-direct.com

The NEO and DANA are small, portable word processors. These machines display a few lines at a time, and the final product can be downloaded onto a personal computer. There also is an add-on text-to-speech program available.

QuickPAD IR

http://www.quickpad.com

The QuickPAD IR is a battery-operated, portable word processor. It uses infrared technology to wirelessly transfer text into another writing application.

HPTouchSmart tx2z series

http://www.shopping.hp.com/series/category/notebooks/tx2z_series/3/
    computer_store?jumpid=reg_R1002_USEN

This is a tablet PC with a diagonal twist screen that accepts input from either a finger or a stylus.

ASSISTIVE TECHNOLOGY: WORD PROCESSING PROGRAMS, DICTIONARIES AND SPELL CHECKERS

Microsoft Office
http://www.office.microsoft.com

This program helps you create documents, PowerPoints, spreadsheets, and databases, and can be run on both a Mac and PC.

Children's Oxford Dictionary & Spell Checker
http://www.franklin.com/estore/dictionary/LWB-1216

This is an electronic dictionary that also includes a thesaurus, spell-correction, calculator, and a variety of games to improve spelling, vocabulary, and math skills.

Spelling Ace & Thesaurus
http://www.franklin.com/estore/dictionary/SA-206S

This electronic dictionary offers phonetic spell correction, as well as synonyms, antonyms, and a personal vocabulary list. It also features a calculator and phone list databank.

ASSISTIVE TECHNOLOGY: KEYBOARDING SKILLS

Type to Learn 4
http://www.sunburst.com

This typing program for all ages, K–12, allows the student to progress at his or her own rate to increase both accuracy and speed. It is available for both Mac and PC, and you can download a 30-day free trial.

Typing Adventure
http://www.typingadventure.com

This is an Internet-based typing program that doesn't require downloads or software. You also can sample this site with a 30-day free home trial.

GS Typing Tutor
http://www.typingstar.com

This downloadable typing program has levels ranging from beginner to experienced. It tracks progress and personalizes review lessons based on your problem keys.

ASSISTIVE TECHNOLOGY: WRITTEN LANGUAGE SOFTWARE

Co:Writer 6

http://www.donjohnston.com/products/cowriter/index.html

Co:Writer is a word prediction software that offers word options based on the first letter or letters the student inputs.

Draft:Builder 6

http://www.donjohnston.com/products/draft_builder/index.html

Draft:Builder breaks down the writing process into easy steps—brainstorming, note-taking, and writing the first draft.

Inspiration and InspireData

http://www.inspiration.com

Inspiration creates graphic organizers on your computer to assist with the writing process. With the click of a mouse, it turns the graphic organizers into outlines. InspireData is used for science, math, and social studies and is a visual way to explore and interpret data. Both can be used on a Mac or PC, and the company offers a downloadable free trial.

ASSISTIVE TECHNOLOGY: TEXT-TO-SPEECH AND SPEECH-TO-TEXT PROGRAMS

Kurzweil 3000

http://kurzweiledu.com

Well-known to many in the dyslexia community, Kurzweil is useful for struggling readers who have difficulty with visual processing. This software reads scanned or downloaded text, and can highlight, annotate, store voice notes, and extract information to create outlines and story guides.

Write:OutLoud 6

http://www.donjohnston.com/products/write_outloud/index.html

Write:OutLoud 6 is a talking word processor that can be used on both Mac and PC. It confirms word choices with the Franklin Talking Spell Checker, homophone checker, and dictionary.

WordQ & SpeakQ

http://www.wordq.com

WordQ provides word prediction with spoken feedback to help you find mistakes. SpeakQ is a speech-to-text program that compliments WordQ. It contains a "speak continuously" mode in which your words are typed directly into a document as you speak.

Dragon NaturallySpeaking 10
http://www.m.nuance.com/dragon-solutions/index.aspx

This software program uses voice recognition to enable you to write documents, e-mails, search the web, and control your PC by speaking.

Macspeech
http://www.macspeech.com

Macspeech is a company that offers a variety of assistive devices for speech-to-text application.

ASSISTIVE TECHNOLOGY: ELECTRONIC READING DEVICES/E-BOOKS

Kindle
http://www.amazon.com/Kindle

The Kindle is a wireless reading device that downloads books and magazines you purchase electronically. Kindle also has a text-to-speech feature.

Sony Reader Digital Books
http://www.sonystyle.com

The Sony Reader Digital Book, Reader Touch Edition™ has a touchscreen display, stylus, and virtual keyboard. The Reader Pocket Edition™ has a 5" display.

eBooks.com
http://www.ebooks.com

This website allows you to download a variety of ebooks onto your computer or even your mobile phone.

Nook
http://www.barnesandnoble.com/nook/?cds2Pid=30919

The Nook has a touchscreen display, virtual keyboard, and wireless connectivity to download books, magazines, or newspapers from Barnes and Noble ebooks.

ASSISTIVE TECHNOLOGY: MATH

MathBits.com
http://www.mathbits.com

This site offers math lessons for secondary and college-level math, as well as computer programming.

Coolmath.com
http://www.coolmath.com

This colorful website includes math lessons and games from prealgebra through geometry.

MathPad Plus by IntelliTools
http://www.intellitools.com

MathPad Plus allows students to do math problems directly on the computer. It is more than a calculator, as problems can include manipulation of fractions and decimals, and can be visually represented with graphics. This device is great for students who have difficulty with pencil and paper.

SENSORY ISSUES

Kranowitz, C. S. (2006). *The out-of-sync child: Recognizing and coping with sensory processing disorder* (Rev. ed.). New York, NY: Perigee Penguin Group.

Although written for adults, this book clearly explains all you wanted to know about sensory processing issues.

Kranowitz, C. S. (2006). *The out-of-sync child has fun: Activities for kids with sensory processing disorder* (Rev. ed.). New York, NY: Perigee Penguin Group.

This book contains fun exercises and strategies to help deal with the difficulties posed by sensory processing issues.

SOCIAL SKILLS AND NONVERBAL COMMUNICATION

Baker, J. (2003). *The social skills picture book: Teaching play, emotion, and communication to children with autism.* Arlington, TX: Future Horizons.

Baker, J. (2006). *The social skills picture book for high school and beyond.* Arlington, TX: Future Horizons.

Both of these books offer annotated photographs of real-life social situations, with options for appropriate reactions.

Baron-Cohen, S. (2004). *Mind reading: The interactive guide to emotions.* London, England: Jessica Kingsley.

This interactive book and DVD-ROM has a library of facial expressions to help students learn to read nonverbal communication. It stars a young Daniel Radcliffe.

Levine, M., & Clutch, J. (2001). *Jarvis Clutch: Social spy.* Cambridge, MA: Educators Publishing Service.

A fun story of the social intricacies of middle school.

Winner, M. G., & Crooke, P. (2008). *You are a social detective!* San Jose, CA: Think Social Publishing.

This entertaining comic book offers insights about "expected" and "unexpected" behaviors and concepts in social interactions.

INTERNET SAFETY

NetSmartz

http://www.netsmartz.org, http://www.netsmartzkids.org, and http://www.nsteens.org

These sites are run by the National Center for Missing and Exploited Children. All of these sites have games, quizzes, video clips, comics, and e-cards, all with the goal of teaching safe habits for the Internet.

Safekids.com

http://www.safekids.com

This site, one of the oldest sites devoted to cybersafety, has a filtered Google search feature, so you don't need to worry that your search will mistakenly take you to an inappropriate site. There also are links to safety tips for kids and teens, including tips about socializing on the web, blogging, and how to recognize the manipulation tactics of child predators.

Wired Kids, Inc.

http://www.wiredkids.org

This site has games to play, quizzes to take, and a wealth of information on how to stay safe online. It even has a report line so that you can "report bad sites, or get advice if you've found something online you don't know how to deal with."

Cyber Treehouse

http://www.cybertreehouse.com

Cyber Treehouse is part of http://www.playitcybersafe.com; both websites are run by the Business Software Alliance. As you climb the cyber treehouse, you can find links to games, videos, and safe sites to visit online.

REFERENCES

American Psychiatric Association. (2000). *Diagnostic and statistical manual of mental disorders* (4th ed., Text rev.). Washington, DC: Author.

Baron-Cohen, S. (2009). *Autism test "could hit maths skills."* Retrieved from http://news.bbc.co.uk/2/hi/health/7736196.stm

Bauman, M. L., & Kemper, T. L. (2004). Neuroanatomic observations of the brain in autism: A review and future directions. *International Journal of Developmental Neuroscience, 23,* 184–186.

Bennet, D. (2009). *Thorkil Sonne: Recruit autistics.* Retrieved from http://www.wired.com/techbiz/people/magazine/17-10/ff_smartlist_sonne

Centers for Disease Control and Prevention. (2007). *Autism spectrum disorders (ASDs).* Retrieved from http://www.cdc.gov/ncbddd/autism/index.html

Centers for Disease Control and Prevention. (2009). *Prevalence of autism spectrum disorders—Autism and developmental disabilities monitoring network, United States, 2006.* Retrieved from http://www.cdc.gov/mmwr/preview/mmwrhtml/ss5810a1.htm

Churcher, S. (2008). *Harry Potter: The brain disorder which means I can't tie my shoelaces.* Retrieved from http://www.dailymail.co.uk/tvshowbiz/

article-1046031/Harry-Pottter-The-brain-disorder-means-I-8217-t-tie-shoelaces.html

Individuals with Disabilities Education Improvement Act, PL 108-446, 118 Stat. 2647 (2004).

Kogan, M. D., Blumberg, S. J., Schieve, L. C., Boyle, C. A., Perrini, J. M., Ghandour, R. M., . . . Van Dyck, P. C. (2009). *Prevalence of parent-reported diagnosis of autism spectrum disorder among children in the US, 2007.* Retrieved from http://pediatrics.aappublications.org/cgi/content/abstract/peds.2009-1522v1

People with autism make more rational decisions, study shows. (2008). Retrieved from http://www.sciencedaily.com/releases/2008/10/081015110228.htm

Rourke, B. P. (Ed.). (1995). *Syndrome of nonverbal learning disabilities: Neurodevelopmental manifestations.* New York, NY: Guilford Press.

Spector, C. C. (2006). *Between the lines: Enhancing inferencing skills.* Eau Claire, WI: Thinking Publications.

Van Reusen, A. K., & Bos, C. (1994). Facilitating student participation in individualized educational programs through motivational strategies and instruction. *Exceptional Children, 22,* 30–32.

Wallis, C. (2009). *For the first time, a census of autistic adults.* Retrieved from http://www.time.com/time/health/article/0,8599,1927415,00.html

BIBLIOGRAPHY

Attwood, T. (1998). *Asperger's syndrome: A guide for parents and professionals.* London, England: Jessica Kingsley.

Dubin, N. (2007). *Asperger syndrome and bullying: Strategies and solutions.* London, England: Jessica Kingsley.

Heinrichs, R. (2003). *Perfect targets: Asperger syndrome and bullying.* Shawnee Mission, KS: Autism Asperger Publishing Company.

Learning Disabilities Association of America. (2004). *Assistive technology (AT) for individuals with learning disabilities.* Retrieved from http://www.ldaamerica.org/pdf/assistive_tech.pdf

Myles, B. S., & Adreon, D. (2001). *Asperger syndrome and adolescence: Practical solutions for school success.* Shawnee Mission, KS: Autism Asperger Publishing Company.

Silverman, S. M., & Weinfeld, R. (2007). *School success for kids with Asperger's syndrome.* Waco, TX: Prufrock Press.

Stewart, K. (2002). *Helping a child with Nonverbal Learning Disorder or Asperger's syndrome: A parent's guide.* Oakland, CA: New Harbinger Publications.

Tanguay, P. B. (2001). *Nonverbal learning disabilities at home: A parent's guide.* London, England: Jessica Kingsley.

Tanguay, P. B. (2002). *Nonverbal learning disabilities at school: Educating students with NLD, Asperger's syndrome, and related conditions.* London, England: Jessica Kingsley.

Thompson, S. (1997). *The source for Nonverbal Learning Disorders.* East Moline, IL: LinguiSystems.

Whitney, R. V. (2000). *The Nonverbal Learning Disorder guide for teachers, parents, employers and therapists* (3rd ed.). San Jose, CA: The Lighthouse Project.

ABOUT THE AUTHORS

Janet Price is the Director of Transition Services for Weinfeld Education Group, LLC, an educational consulting group in the Washington, DC area. She also is the parent of a teenager diagnosed with Nonverbal Learning Disorder. Janet holds a bachelor's degree in international affairs from The George Washington University. After a decade of service in the U.S. State Department, Janet found a new use for her skills in diplomacy and negotiation as she began to advocate for services in the public school system for her child's little understood learning profile. As an educational consultant, Janet now helps other families do the same. Janet moderates an Internet forum for people with NLD and their families at http://www.delphiforums.com. She writes a special education column at http://www.examiner.com/x-26267-Montgomery-County-Special-Education-Examiner. Janet lives with her husband, two children, and an overweight Shih Tzu in suburban Maryland.

Jennifer Engel Fisher, M.Ed., is the Assistant Director of Weinfeld Education Group, LLC, an educational consulting group in the Washington, DC, area. Jennifer earned her bachelor's degree in psychology from the University of Maryland, Baltimore County, and her master's degree in special education from The Johns Hopkins University. Jennifer's consulting practice involves working with families of special needs children in a variety of ways, including advocacy, training, and organizational coaching for those with executive functioning issues. She currently teaches the Special Needs Advocacy Training Institute in Maryland. Jennifer has been a special education teacher in both inclusion and self-contained classrooms that served a variety of populations, including persons with autism spectrum disorders, ADHD, and learning disabilities. Jennifer also was a learning specialist at a private school in Washington, DC. She is a contributing author to the best-selling *School Success for Kids With ADHD*, also published by Prufrock Press. Jennifer lives with her husband and two children outside of Washington, DC.